One Hundred Tales of the Settle-Carlisle Railway

*Some other Settle-Carlisle
Books by W R Mitchell:*

THE LONG DRAG (1962)
SETTLE-CARLISLE RAILWAY –
   with David Joy (1966)
SETTLE-CARLISLE CENTENARY –
   with David Joy (1975)
THE RAILWAY SHANTIES –
   Settle and District Civic Society (1975)
SEVEN YEARS HARD –
   with Nigel Mussett (1976)
SETTLE TO CARLISLE –
   with David Joy (1982)
LIFE ON THE SETTLE-CARLISLE RAILWAY (1984)
MEN OF THE SETTLE-CARLISLE (1985)
WALKS FROM THE SETTLE-CARLISLE RAILWAY –
   with R W Swallow (1987)
SHANTY LIFE ON THE SETTLE-CARLISLE RAILWAY (1988)
HOW THEY BUILT THE SETTLE-CARLISLE RAILWAY (1989)
FOOTPLATE TALES OF THE SETTLE-CARLISLE RAILWAY –
   with Peter Fox (1990)
THE STORY OF RIBBLEHEAD VIADUCT (1990)
GHOSTS OF THE SETTLE-CARLISLE –
   with Peter Fox (1990)
GARSDALE AND AISGILL –
   with Peter Fox (1990)
HELLIFIELD AND THE RAILWAY (1991)
LOCOMOTIVES SEEN ON THE SETTLE-CARLISLE –
   with Peter Fox (1992)
RIBBLEHEAD RE-BORN (1992)
THE MEN WHO MADE THE SETTLE-CARLISLE (1993)
DENT – highest station (1995)
*THE LOST SHANTIES OF RIBBLEHEAD (1996)
CELEBRATION 10 –
   with Settle-Carlisle Business Liaison Group (1996)
*GARSDALE – History and Traditions of a Junction Station (1999)

Copies still available

One Hundred Tales of the Settle-Carlisle Railway

by W R Mitchell

Illustrated by Peter Fox

CASTLEBERG
2000

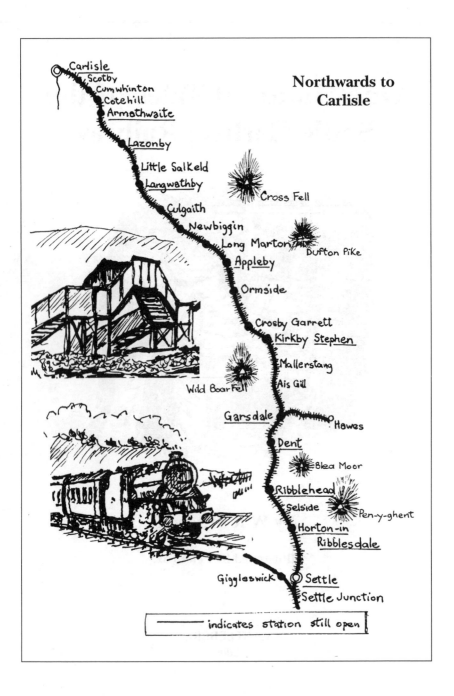

Northwards to Carlisle

Carlisle
Scotby
Cumwhinton
Cotehill
Armathwaite
Lazonby
Little Salkeld
Langwathby
Culgaith
Newbiggin
Long Marton
Appleby
Ormside
Crosby Garrett
Kirkby Stephen
Mallerstang
Ais Gill
Garsdale
Dent
Ribblehead
Selside
Horton-in-Ribblesdale
Gigglewick
Settle
Settle Junction

Cross Fell
Dufton Pike
Wild Boar Fell
Hawes
Blea Moor
Pen-y-ghent

—— indicates station still open

Contents

Introduction	5
Hellifield	29
Settle Junction	33
Settle	35
Stainforth	37
Helwith Bridge	39
Horton-in-Ribblesdale	39
Selside	51
Salt Lake	53
Ribblehead	54
Ribblehead Viaduct	57
Blea Moor	60
Blea Moor Tunnel	65
Dent Head	69
Dent Station	70
Garsdale Water Toughs	74
Garsdale and Hawes	76
Hawes	79
Aisgill	89
Mallerstang	91
The Eden Valley	92
Kirkby Stephen	93
Crosby Garrett	94
Appleby	95
Griseburn Ballast Sidings	98
Newbiggin	100
Culgaith	100
Long Meg	101
Lazonby Sand Hole	102
Lazonby and Kirkoswald	102
Armathwaite	106
Low House Crossing	106
Cumwhinton	106
Carlisle	107

Acknowledgements to railmen and their families, past and present:
W C Addy, Harry Cox, Alan Dugdale, John Duncan,
Norman Dobson, Nancy Edmondson, Fred Edwards,
Richard (Dick) Fawcett, Jimmy Fishwick, Tony Freschini,
Brian Hayton, George Horner, R D Ledbetter, Jimmy McClelland,
Jack Sedgwick, Derek Soames, James M Taylor, David Tibbetts.
Also to Bob Swallow, for his inspiration and guidance.

A **Castleberg** Book.

First published in the United Kingdom in 2000.

Text, © W R Mitchell 2000.

The moral right of the author has been asserted.

ISBN 1 871064 49 X

Typeset in New Baskerville, printed and bound in the United Kingdom by
Lamberts Print & Design, Station Road, Settle, North Yorkshire, BD24 9AA.

Published by Castleberg, 18 Yealand Avenue, Giggleswick, Settle,
North Yorkshire, BD24 0AY.

Foreword
by Ann Cryer, M.P.

When Bill Mitchell asked me to write a "short foreword" for his collection of tales of the Settle to Carlisle Railway I thought it would be difficult. Once I started making notes on memories of this wonderful line and the connected bits of my life, I realised that the problem would really be too much to say, therefore I've had to be quite disciplined and keep my recollections to but a few.

Two weeks before I married my late husband Bob Cryer in August 1963, we joined a ramblers' special train, Bob from Saltaire, myself from Blackburn, joining up at Skipton to be put down at Horton-in-Ribblesdale, for our very pleasant walk and lunch at an extremely old farmhouse on a bend in the road. This was my introduction to a line that became a continuing feature of our lives together, second only to the Worth Valley branch of which he was the founder, chairman and for the first twelve years of the preservation society did just about every job that was needed.

The Settle to Carlisle line was on the other hand a source of great pleasure of a more relaxed nature. Trips to Carlisle for the day, just for the joy of the experience. An extremely pleasant memory is of taking John and Jane, our children, on a Dalesrail ramblers' day out, leaving the train at, I believe, Langwathby and going by minibus to Keswick for a round Derwentwater guided walk.

In 1973, the day my father died, I hurried over to be with him. However on that very bleak day my spirits were lifted a little by Bob's account of a long meeting with Doug Smith of BBC TV Leeds, discussing Bob's script for a half hour documentary, *Settle to Carlisle – the last main line to Scotland*, which he also narrated.

The cameraman was Keith Massey and the editor Ted Croot. For a few weeks that summer John, Jane and I travelled to various locations on the line, whilst Bob decided on best vantage points for various shots. We also visited Derby Museum on a wet Sunday, to use their excellent models and lay-outs for a mock-up of an accident near Hawes junction in 1910. The three of us became part of the crew, carrying and holding lights. Bob was extremely proud of this documentary and with good reason. The modest fee he earned paid for the four of us to have a return trip to Carlisle with the very great luxury of lunch on board. I would dearly love a video of that film!

Bill Mitchell gave me a selection of the "One Hundred Tales" to give me an idea of the book, and what an extremely enjoyable read they all are. My favourite is the Selside tale, "Women in Charge." I laughed out loud, which was a little awkward since I was writing and reading in the seriously thoughtful atmosphere of the House of Commons library. A female colleague sitting next to me also appreciated the story.

Bill Mitchell's much earlier book *Settle-Carlisle Railway,* sub-titled *The Midland Record-breaking Route to Scotland* has had pride of place on our bookshelves since published jointly with David Joy in 1966. Judging by the ballpoint markings Bob must have referred to it for his documentary. There was a time when we thought that the book, empty track-bed and sad derelict stations, would be our only reminders of this wonderful piece of civil engineering achievement. Thanks to the determined eight year long fight-back against closure proposals by rail users, enthusiasts, Parliamentarians and Councillors (as documented in James Towler's *The Battle for the Settle and Carlisle*), this amazing example of man's mastery of his environment is now preserved for (I hope) posterity. This book is a further celebration of a much-loved railway and the men and women who created, maintained and ran services over it.

Finally, I pay tribute to the band of volunteers who continue to generate enthusiasm for the line by their own example and imagination through "The Friends of the Settle and Carlisle Line." Long may they continue.

Ann Cryer is MP for Keighley, President of the Keighley and Worth Valley Railway Preservation Society and a Vice President of the Friends of the Settle and Carlisle Line.

Introduction

Our cover picture is one of a series of cartoons drawn by Jos Armitage, best-known as Ionicus. It portrays a decrepit railway station, occupied only by two tramps, one of whom tells the other "and now they have a train that will do 120 miles an hour." In the 1980s, we had a terrible feeling that the Settle-Carlisle would be closed or, at least, reduced to branch lines, with a railwayless gap in the middle. Some of the stations had already closed and become derelict, as Ionicus portrayed.

April 11, 1989, will go down in the history of the Settle-Carlisle as the day on which the Transport Minister ruled out the expected private take over of the line. He encouraged private interest but instructed British Rail to continue to operate it. Many of those who had fought for six years in the longest-running and most costly railway closure attempt to be mounted felt that the voice of the people had been heard in the corridors of power. Flags were flown in celebration. The Friends of the Settle-Carlisle line developed the positive role of giving publicity to the line to encourage more people to use it.

Today, the surviving stations are immaculate, large sums of money are being spent by Railtrack on new track and new platforms to conform to modern passenger stock. A steam-special brings an occasional glamorous touch. Freight traffic, mainly coal and gypsum, helps to polish the tracks.

The Settle-Carlisle, constructed between 1869 and 1876 with the aid of up to 6,000 navvies and in a period of especially inclement weather, was a bid by the young and thrustful Midland Company for a share in the lucrative Scottish traffic. Despite mountainous terrain, it was devised as a fast, all-weather route, the engineers making clever use of two north-south valleys, Ribblesdale and the Eden Valley. Awesome engineering problems were encountered and overcome with confidence and verve in the high Pennine country lying between the dales.

What the Midland and its men created, another army of workers sustained. The tales in this book are about some of them. The heroes were the footplate men on the steam locomotives, for did not every small boy want to be an engine-driver? The unsung heroes were those who maintained the track, including the ganger whose length was still good fifteen years after he had retired. "The next length was knocked to pieces." Among those who died were a few firemen who, on looking out of a train as it neared Carlisle, cracked their heads on the London Road bridge.

My book will help to revive memories of "working steam," when the Long Drag, those 22 miles from Settle Junction to the peak of the railway, tested the skill of the footplate men, whose worst crime was to "run out of steam." Little has been written about the Drag for traffic going south – the steady climb from Kirkby Stephen through Mallerstang to Aisgill. Brian Hayton, a driver who had been passed out "for steam" by the legendary George Gordon, told me: "You had a big dip to Ormside viaduct, then it was up, up by Crosby Garrett. There was a little bit o' level at Griseburn. You went around by the viaduct, then you were up again – through Kirkby Stephen and Birkett Tunnel. When you got to Mallerstang, if you were hard up for a bit o' steam the driver used to shut off and you took advantage of a little bit o' level and a dip to get a bit more steam. Then you made your final effort up to the summit, looking out for the distant signal that was called, by relieved crews, The Star of Bethlehem."

The first time Brian went that way he was booked with an old chap called Percy Houlder, who'd been a fireman at Durran Hill. "He used to tell me that when he went up Mallerstang valley on a winter's night, at two, three or four o'clock, he'd seen lights in cottages and farm houses. I once asked why people should be out of bed at such times. Percy said the Midland Railway had given these people a paraffin allowance to keep a light on in case there was a mishap on the line. It must have been introduced after the Aisgill crash, when one train ran into the back of another."

The Settle-Carlisle is well-documented. My own interest has been in folk tales, which must be recorded if they are to survive. For half a century I have enjoyed the company of drivers, firemen, signalmen, stationmasters, porters, goods clerks and permanent way men whose skill has kept the line operating. Here is a selection of stories which put some flesh on the bare bones of statistics.

Footplate Men

The number of men who have occupied the footplate during the days of "working steam" is now small. They make light of the difficulties. They had gulped down sandwiches in brief interludes between operating the engine; they kept a bottle or can of tea warm on a Derby engine by placing it on a loop formed of pipes that supplied steam to the sanding gear. Spending much of their working lives with their heads and upper bodies outside the cab, as they looked into a searching wind and driving rain, it was astonishing they had nothing more serious than aching shoulders in later life. "In winter time, some of those top drivers wore one or two top coats and a muffler. They had their caps pulled well down over their ears."

They were characters to a man, including a Holbeck chap with the strange nickname of Pamma Jamma. The ex-driver who told me about him said "tha can spell it how tha likes" and added that he was rarely clean and tidy when at work. Not long after coming on duty he looked as though he'd been up t'chimney. In contrast was John Silverwood, a Leeds driver, "a gentleman through and through," who kept his overalls spotlessly clean and well-creased (he never sat down!).

Immaculate John was said to be "a flower-man," whereas his usually-grimy brother, who worked locos out of Stourton depot was "a vegetable man!" John was also an outstanding engineman who would set the regulator in such a way that every trip was relatively easy. He had a nimble mind. At Carlisle barracks [lodgings for railmen] he enjoyed the company of footplate men because then he could exercise and enlarge his wide knowledge of dialect. At Carlisle, English crews socialised with Scottish crews and most of the Scottish dialects might be heard. John Silverwood would quietly identify their precise origins within Scotland. He might address an individual in his own dialect.

One of the Leeds drivers who was "a bit of a character" at Holbeck is recalled by a Carlisle man who reported at ten o'clock at night for cleaning duties. "The foreman came to us and said: 'Go down to the station. A fireman's gone sick. Work with the driver to Leeds'. When the train came in, it was a Scot. I'd heard about this fella before. Driver Crawley was four foot nothing. His fireman, who was called Big Arthur, stood nearly seven foot in his stockinged feet. The fireman got off the train. I said: 'What's the matter, Arthur?' He said: 'It's him. I'll fill the tank and put a good fire on for you – and good luck to you'."

Driver Crawley ranted and raved. It was winter-time and he had long leather boots, such as were worn by despatch riders in the war. "We set off, round by London road and before long I thought I'd been through a mangle. Jeeze. Sparks were coming out of that Scot! We got to Leeds. He shook my hand, patted me on the back, and asked me what I had come up for. I said: 'Ten o' clock cleaner'. Driver Crawley said: 'You've done well. Get yourself on that Carlisle train. I'll take the engine back to Holbeck misself. (A pause). Poor little fellow, when he retired, he was crossing the road when he got knocked down by a bus and killed. He was quite a man. Could he 'crack' an engine!"

You got good jobs – and bad jobs. Brian Hayton remembers how elated he felt when as a young fireman he worked with Joe Stobbart, a top-flight driver. "It was great. I was twenty-one years old, firing on a Duchess. I thought I was King Dick." Firing was an art for unless it was done with an understanding of the type of engine you could make a real mess of it. "The big Duchess steamed better if coal was placed round the back corners. You soon knew if the coal wasn't burning properly. Your steam started to flag."

The fireman had a big clinker shovel and a rake, which "had a V at the end to slide over the top of the bars. If you started firing it wrong, and coal landed in the middle or you were not getting it to the fore-end, or if there was too much to the fore-end, you took the rake and worked it. When you pulled the rake out it was red-hot. You had to be careful you didn't burn your hand, which you did sometimes."

As a fireman, Bill Addy of Leeds experienced the extremes of temperature in winter. He fired engines while wearing his heavy railway macintosh. "The heat of the fire was fantastic. I was scorched on one side and frozen on the other. There was ice on the bucket a matter of only eight feet from the firebox. You try firing with a mac on and the rain washing the muck and slurry as well as cobs of coal down the tender."

On some big engines, such as Crabs, the firebox door was of the sliding variety, controlled by a handle. So the driver stood with one hand on the regulator and the other operating the door. "As soon as you'd drawn out the shovel, he'd shut it. He was not letting cold air as well as rain get into the fire!"

All Sorts of Coal

Coal and steam! These were the main elements in operating the line. Coal was a "mixed grill." A lot of it was rubbish. A party who travelled light-engine to Blea Moor for snow ploughing had dirty coal and the first job on arrival was to clean out the fire. "To look at that coal, you'd think it was slate. We called it 'legs and arms' because it came in long slabs. When you hit it with a hammer, it was so brittle it broke up in layers. Put it in t'fire, and it crackled. You see see bits flying off it."

Wigan coal imparted much heat but tended to run, clogging the bars of the firebox. A knowing fireman spread some loose limestone or grit on the bars at the start of his term of duty. The so-called Yorkshire Hards sizzled but produced tremendous heat. When used by signalmen it burnt so fiercely it was responsible for gutting one or two signal boxes. The choicest coal, kept for the passenger trains, was Yorkshire Main, which was "hard as iron but marvellous stuff to use. Some of the lumps of coal that came off Leeds were like tombstones.

GANGER'S TIME-BOOK.

from _14_ m. _20_ ch., to _16_ m. _10_ ch.

For Week ending _____

NAME.	OCCUPATION		F.
Mason Thomas	Ganger	2/	1
Fothergill John	under		1
Clarke Joseph	Lab	2/	1
Flack George No 2	"	2/	1
Stevenson William	"		1
Johnston Andrew	" about		1
		_11_	
		W 8	
Mason Thomas	Ganger	2/	1
Fothergill John	under		1
Clarke Joseph	Lab	2/	1
Flack George No 2	"	2/	½
Stevenson William	"		1
Johnston Andrew	"		1

Settle & Carlisle BRANCH.   E. B. 10.

April 1ˢᵗ 1886

Bemrose & Sons, Printers, 23, Old Bailey, London; and Derby.

S.	Sun	M.	T.	W.	T.	Total Days	Rate.				REMARKS.
1		1	1	1	1	6	4/6	1	7	1	Repairing
1		1	1	1	1	6	3/8	1	2		Permanent
1		1	1	1	1	6	3/4	1		1	Way
1		1	1	1	1	6	"	1		1	"
1		1	1	1	1	6	"	1		1	"
1		1	1	1	1	6	"	1		1	"
								6	9		Pay at Ribble...

April 15 1886

1		1	1	1	1	6	4/6	1	7		Repairing
1		1	1	1	1	6	3/8	1	2		Permanent
1		1	1	1	1	6	3/4	1			Way
1		1	1	1	1	5½	"		18	4	"
1		1	1	1	1	6	"	1			"
1		1	1	1	1	6	"	1			"
								6	7	4	Pay at P...hea...

You had to set to with the pick and get cracking and break it up and throw it in."

A Carlisle driver told me that Scotch coal was not very good. Most Welsh coal was, according to the same railman, "only fit for hurling from trains. We chucked bits of coal at rabbits – and if a man scored a hit, he'd nip off the train and collect them." An enterprising farmer in the Eden Valley set up a scarecrow near the tracks. It was a tempting target for a fireman who used a lump of coal as a missile. The man had abundant coal – for nothing.

During the Second World War, when the black-out had to be observed, and heavy sheets were provided so that the glow of the fire could not be seen from the air, the footplate men were literally working in a tent. The first instruction was to put the sheets on both night and day.

Cabin Life

Many amusing tales emanated from the lineside cabins that were used by platelayers, the cabins being spaced at intervals of about a quarter of a mile. A maintenance gang used the nearest cabin at meal-times and during bad weather. The men did not work in the rain. "If it was chucking it down, they slunk about in t'cabin all day." There were cabins and cabins, "the warmest little places you ever experienced." In the main, the cabins by the Drag were "little poor 'uns" compared with those on the Morecambe line.

Some cabins were stone-built but the majority were formed of sleeper-wood, having good hard wooden tops covered with felt that was tarred. So much tar had been spread over some huts during the years that in hot weather it was inclined to run. The inside of a cabin was always lime-washed. Wooden cabins were warmest. In winter, the men didn't turn it till it was proper light. In the shortest days of winter they were in again by half past three.

A cabin was well-aired. The men knew in advance where they would be and ensured that a few days before they moved a fire would be lit in the nearest cabin to take away the chill. "Wherever there was a cabin there was a platelayer. He was there forty minutes before he need be. He'd have a big fire going. The stove was of the square variety, with a lile flap in the front."

There was always a little desk under the window. A cupboard in one corner held the tools. Home-made benches, probably sleepers on edge, were arranged round the side of the cabin. The benches had headrests so that the men might lie down. But mainly they sat round the stove, boiled water in a kettle, warmed a pie – and, opening the flap, spat into the fire. "Up Dent way, it was entertaining to a newcomer to listen to the men yarning."

The ganger picked the best seat, though he hadn't much time to loll about, for he'd to "look t'length" each morning. In the cabin, as the ganger got soaked by rain, the men smoked black twist. "The atmosphere was generally pretty thick." Or they played "nap," a favourite card game. If they gambled, it was only for pennies. Some men slept and snored.

A gang consisted of five men, including the ganger. Some cabins were named after t'ganger. They included Adam's Cabin, Tom's Cabin and Ted's Cabin (Ted was a brother of Tom). Adam Rudd, the ganger on t'Hawes branch, was "a big fella who reared up to nothing." Another was named Gangsters' Cabin, from some ancient joke that no one could recall.

The most celebrated was Hangman's Cabin, in Mallerstang, named because a man who had become thoroughly depressed hanged himself. A fellow platelayer found him and cut him down. Not long afterwards, the cabin was demolished, according to one story. A more authentic tale is that it was fired by sparks from a steam-special. (The story of Hangman's Cabin would be wrongly associated by some writers with a nearby wooden bridge, which became Hangman's Bridge. Though no human tragedy occurred here, it was used by a local farmer to dispose of dead sheep. He was seen dragging a dead animal on to the bridge, lifting a loose board and squeezing the sheep through the gap. It fell on to the track. The farmer claimed compensation from the railway company.

Characters All

In the inter-war years, Norman Dobson worked on the northern stretches of the line and was a fund of railway stories. So was Richard Fawcett, who wrote a book about his railway experiences. During one of our chats, he told me about Mickey Mouse, the nickname of an inspector who crept down ditches in a bid to snoop on a gang of railwaymen. "There were men everywhere. Ten men with bars; twenty men for lifting the rails with 'dogs' and thirty for loading rails on to the wagons when they had been freed. Re-ballasting jobs were done by men wielding picks and shovels."

Norman told of German Jack, a railwayman employed at Appleby until 1914 when his tongue ran away with him and he was interned. Bill Wilson of Appleby, ganger of the Extra Gang, who retired in 1927, was among those who attended when the engine of a ballast train was de-railed in the main line crossover at Crosby Garrett. Bill used a stack of fish-plates as the fulcrum and a 30 ft rail as the level to slip the engine back into place. With one end of the rail under the centre of the bogie axle, and the gang weighing on the rail, a few concerted jerks eased the wheels up. Then, with a snatch and a twist, the job was done.

Red for Danger

The signalmen maintained many a solitary, but rarely a lonely, vigil. Richard Fawcett would "look out in the half-light in spring and see foxes running about with their cubs. I'd sit of a summer's night and hear the curlews calling. They didn't seem to go to sleep. In winter, I'd hear foxes screaming as they courted down in the woods." The men who had a "balmy air" on the Morecambe line would plug in "and hear the Settle-Carlisle men panicking when a heavy snowfall was expected."

During the Second World War, when a "red alert" halted traffic on the line, one signalman turned down t'lamp, lay down in t'box – and dreamt he was in a local wood, rabbiting. During the same period, "something peculiar" happened at Griseburn box on a Saturday evening every few weeks. The lamp in the "down" distant signal would go out. The signalman on duty, quite properly in the circumstances, called out a permanent way man to collect a trimmed and ready-lit spare lamp from the signalman.

The p.w. man claimed the minimum two hours. He earned even more when an emergency call came during the hallowed hours between midnight on Saturday and midnight on Sunday. It was too much of a good thing. Those concerned were alerted. The Stationmaster ensured that in future the signal was provided with Long Life paraffin.

A signalman on the Drag became an authority on Hot Axle Boxes. A wagon wheel was solid on its axle; the whole lot turned, and an axle box was in two halves, fastened up with bolts. If there was a divided box, where a bolt came loose and the lower half fell away, it took with it the oily pad that provided lubrication. The box would get so hot it struck fire. When a box burnt out, the next stage was a "squealer." Now the defect could be heard as well as seen. It was vital to report it immediately or the wagon would drop on to the wheel and possibly de-rail the train.

Richard Fawcett, who had been platelayer and guard and spent his later years as a signalman on the Morecambe line, told me: "You can't imagine the romantic nights we had at one or two o'clock in the morning in winter. There was a system of telephones that reached from Lancaster to Hellifield South." If the bosses were not about, by adjusting a plug, the system could be connected with Keighley. "If they had all put their plugs in we could have talked to London if we'd wanted."

The telephones would be switched through and the "lads" chattered away over a big area. "There would be Settle-Carlisle lads talking, as far as Appleby. On a good night, men as far away as Leeds and Goole would also be listening in to us Dales lads. To them, we were outlandish. I remember a heck of a row on t'telephone. Someone said: 'Shut up – there's a bit o' good coming now'! He'd switched

Green Ayre locomotive to Belfast locomotive and there was a row about delivering spare parts."

Richard himself told his tales about poaching. "They all loved it. You know, there wasn't a dull moment. One night we even talked about the size of women's shoes and came to the conclusion that no woman was worth picking up who had a shoe size of less than six. One signalman who agreed said: 'My missus takes a four and she's pretty bad-tempered.' Another said: 'My old lass is aw reight – she takes a six'." The signalman at Settle Junction, Jimmy Evans, would not join in with us to talk, but he'd listen. "We called him Old Silent."

The night's telephone hook-up would stop immediately if someone reported a mishap, such as a derailment. Someone was in trouble. Immediately, every plug was pulled out and normal telephone service was resumed.

"Limey" and "Lodger"

The Settle-Carlisle traffic included freight trains with special names, such as Limey, an evening train that collected lime from the quarries of North Ribblesdale and took it up into Scotland. A freight train from Carlisle to Leeds was called Lodger because the crew lodged in Leeds and "fetched" the train back on the following day. Perhaps the most celebrated was Bonnyface, the "lile passenger train" that went to Hawes. Those who speculate on the name usually conclude it was so called because on its return trip, in the late afternoon, it indicated to the permanent way men it was almost time to knock-off work.

There was informality in the way goods trains would make unscheduled stops to pick up signalmen who were marooned at places like Blea Moor by grim weather. At times, they might stop to collect the heavily pregnant or ailing wife or child of a railman. During the 1947 blizzard, a schoolmistress habitually travelled on the footplate of a goods train from temperate Settle to alpine Horton-in-Ribblesdale.

The top engine drivers on the Midland had their names on a board that fitted into brackets on the outside of the cab. By the time a man reached this status, he knew all the dodges. On his last day at work, before retirement, one driver pulled up at Appleby North and made a great show of walking around the engine, feeling the boxes. He then came up the box steps and asked the signalman to tell Control that the train would have to crawl down to Carlisle because he had a hot-box. Control said: "At least it'll be his last." As for the driver, he told his mates, with a wink: "Did yer ivver see such bad luck on me last day, an aw?"

The Settle-Carlisle was really the Leeds-Carlisle. Many locos were stabled at Leeds. Albert Wilcock, who was a fireman at the Stourton shed, which supplied freight locomotives for the Settle-Carlisle road, recalls that rape, a fine vegetable oil, was used to fuel the lamps used at night-time. This was vital if the fireman was to see clearly when using the injectors that kept the boiler supplied with water.

Rape-oil was unofficially used for the traditional "fry-up" on the shovel when a crew was side-tracked for a long period to keep the road open for faster traffic. "Then you would slake down the shovel with the fizzle pipe that supplied hot water direct from the boiler. You'd pour on some rape-oil and add fried bread, eggs and bacon. I can taste it now. The trouble was it became so popular that folk were taking oil home for domestic use. The railway authorities introduced blended burning oil, which was 'horrible'."

Funny Weather

The chief enemy of the Settle-Carlisle was the weather. In the days of steam freight locomotives, which lacked side doors, the firemen had to cope with the ravages of the Helm Wind, which rampaged along the eastern side of Edenvale and was reputedly so strong it blew t'nebs off t'geese that were grazing on a village green. More to the point, it was known to blow coal from a shovel as the fireman was transferring it from tender to firebox.

A Carlisle man who began work on the railway at Durranhill in 1917 told me his first "firing" job was with Bob Newbould, a main line driver aged seventy-three. At times, when t'Helm was blowing, he had

In answer to your

In your reply refer to

187808.
192308

Mr Crossley
Dent

Dear Sir
Snow Storm

I am glad to find
that you and your wife did
all you possibly could for
the comfort of the passengers
who were delayed by the Snow
storm, and it was gratifying
to hear the accounts of your
exertions. I am very pleased
with what you did, and have

pleasure in sending you a
cheque for £5, - £3 in payment
of the enclosed account and
£2 as a gratuity for your
-self and your wife.

Please acknowledge, and
return the account receipted.

I shall also record the
circumstances on your pedigree.

Yours truly.

Cheltenham

to wait until the train entered a cutting before he could replenish the fire.

During the Victorian construction days, boulder clay had been hard as concrete in dry weather and as tricky as treacle when soaked. Long after the line was opened, this geological mush remained a problem. The embankments and cuttings were slow to settle down, creating work for the Slip and Drainage Gangs. At Dent, a "snow fence" made of old railway sleepers was effective for a time.

In a prolonged snowtime, as in 1947 and 1963, the cutting in which Dent station stood was soon filled in. When snow was forecast, locomotives with ploughs, based at Hellifield or Carlisle, were sent to keep the lines open. At one time a ploughing unit consisted of two engines, back to back, with an old brake van in the middle. Men who had an uneasy feeling that in a smash-up they would be squashed in the middle demanded that a pug engine should be used in between.

Ordinary nose ploughs were in use. The back engine was sheeted so that snow would be thrown clear of the cab. A big drift might be 500 yards long, which meant that the outfit was backed for half a mile and then driven furiously at the drift. The impact was something similar to having hit a brick wall. A Skipton driver remarked: "If you hit a right bad drift, you got a wobble on!"

Often the plough came to a juddering halt. "You reversed and tried again till you got through." It was terrifying, especially in daylight. "As the snow got deeper you could hear it scratching on the engine. Then the snow came in, between the floorboards of the cab, into every nook and cranny. It packed so far, the engine became belly-bound. The wheels began to spin. You could be standing on the footplate, up to your waist in snow."

Brian Hayton says: "I've never been stuck in snow, luckily, but I've ploughed through some big drifts. It was a thankless job. You'd to stand, get a head of steam, make a charge at the drift. When you hit a drift, the snow came across the top of the engine. If there wasn't a cab sheet, it came into the cab. It fell in the tender. Your coal was soaking wet. You were shovelling snow. If you had been out with the plough for a while, your fire was dull. Snow got into your boots. It was a really unpleasant task." Eventually, the tender of a snow plough was provided with a big wooden cover to separate the coal from the snow.

A train buried in Shale Cutting at Dent – "where t'first and last flakes o' snow seemed to land" – was re-discovered when several men were walking that way on a snow-clearing job and one of them fell through the locomotive roof light. The driver had left it open. "It was quite funny, really."

All Change

Came the diesels. With a steam locomotive, the harder it is driven the more power it generates. When you shut the regulator, the boiler starts to go down in output. It's always there when you need it and it is accustomed to be worked with intermittent full power and shut-off. Arguably, it is more suited to railway working than the diesel.

As diesel trains were introduced to the Settle-Carlisle, they were maintained initially in the damp and grimy depots built for steam traction. Problems occurred, as with any other novelty. A diesel engine works well under continuing full power, as on a generator. When used for diesel traction, there are variations related to the track, the speed and the load. From being on full power, the engine suddenly drops to idling speeds. This did not suit the early diesel engines; neither does it entirely suit the diesel today.

A man with a special insight into the introduction of diesel traction on the Settle-Carlisle is John Duncan, who entered railway service in 1948 as an apprentice engineer at Gorton, Manchester, and who twenty years later became maintenance foreman at the new diesel depot at Carlisle.

The first time he went on the Settle-Carlisle was in 1941. During the war, servicemen were told which routes they must take. John was with his father, whose ship lay at West Hartlepool, and the Settle-Carlisle was joined at Hellifield for Garsdale, where they changed to the Wensleydale line to Northallerton. Subsequently, John got to know the Settle-Carlisle well, for from 1968 it was the line on which Type 4

English Electric-type, the early diesel locomotives, were tested after being under repair. A locomotive was attached to the front of a thousand-ton freight train to be driven to Aisgill summit. From Appleby onwards, full power could be maintained and checks made.

"We had a lot of problems in the early days with over-heating. The fault lay in the radiators." Two double-bank radiators lay on each side with a baffle plate in the middle. The baffle corroded and was bypassed by the water. A lot of engines had to be taken off with high water temperature at Howe and Company sidings, not far from the city. When sorting out the problem, a pigmy light bulb was attached to a long rod to investigate the piping. "We started by having the radiators repaired at Crewe and then the works here got round to supplying complete radiator sets, which we just changed. Gradually we worked through the fleet."

In the early days, electrical troubles arose, partly from the unfamiliarity of maintenance staff with aspects of the new equipment. They were quick to learn. Some of the older drivers who were accustomed to looking down the side of a locomotive became sick when they found themselves sitting in a bow-fronted cab with the rails rushing up at them. A small number was taken off driving duties. Complaints were received about certain small but important mechanical aspects, such as defective window-wipers.

An early diesel locomotive on the Settle-Carlisle was the Crossley, Type 2, working the Condor from Cricklewood to Glasgow. Then gradually, steam traction was replaced by the Sultzer Crompton Parkinsons, Type 4. Later, it was the Class 47, a mixed traffic engine that was the workhorse for a long period. This was mainly because a great many were built. Having been devised and constructed in a hurry, there were design faults. Consequently, as a locomotive the Class 47 could not be rated too highly unless those who ran it were prepared to spend a good deal of money to maintain it. The Class 50, an English Electric product with a large engine for those early days, was also seen on the Settle-Carlisle.

Now with the Class 60, which gives plenty of power, the driver's skill is in applying it to the rails. Old photographs of the Settle-Carlisle show an absence of trees from railway property. Then the inclination was to let trees develop. The sycamore, which grows rapidly, was soon asserting itself. The horse chestnut, another tree with a large leaf, was to prove an irritant in autumn, when cast leaves fell on the tracks, many to be crushed. In effect, they lubricated the line, causing engine wheels to skid.

What of the "steam men," who had to switch to the new-fangled diesel? Jimmy Fishwick, training on diesels after long years on the footplate, met a driver from Hull who, after traversing the Settle-Carlisle, said: "If I'd been made a fireman over this road, I'd have given my notice." Yet if one of the early diesels broke down – which was not infrequently the case when they were introduced – the inclination was to resort to steam.

"The old steam-drivers didn't like these novel gadgets. They were quite happy with a steam engine. In the diesel you were sitting on your behind for mile after mile, and it seemed boring, but they soon got into the new ways." Their wives were happy, for their menfolk could go to work wearing decent clothes and in the knowledge they would not return in a thoroughly mucky state.

Steam Specials

Diesels may rule the Settle-Carlisle, but the glamour trains are the "steam specials." The old dependence on good coal began to apply again. On the day the locomotive was *Blue Peter*, a helicopter flew above it, recording a magnificent journey. On the way from Blackburn, the footplate crew struggled for steam because of poor coal. A search went on in the tender for some better coal. The steam began to "come round" and by the time Blea Moor was reached the crew was happy again. At Garsdale, about seventeen minutes had been lost.

When the *Flying Scotsman* was en route from Blackburn to Carlisle, water was being lost. By the time the train was passing through Dent, it dawned on the crew that the tank might be empty. When the train stopped at Garsdale, the lad with the tanker was invited to climb on the tender and look into the tank. It was bone dry. It had been so all the way from Dent. An official who inquired about it remarked, somewhat naively: "That was a bit tight, wasn't it?"

Epilogue

For a time, the Settle-Carlisle looked forlorn. A former goods clerk, visiting Settle station yard after some years, found it had changed out of recognition. "Just about everything I remembered had been demolished. There were wire fences, new buildings. I saw an old railway pal; he said – 'Ay, lad: are you thinking t'same as me? That it's all bin a waste o' time'."

Today, with the railway authority working in conjunction with the Friends of the Settle-Carlisle line, the stations of the celebrated railway are as smart as they ever were and millions of pounds are being spent on restoring the track.

Hellifield

When the "Little" North Western Railway arrived at Hellifield in 1846, the station that was built at the edge of this quiet little village was less important than Bell Busk or Long Preston. The arrival of the Lancashire and Yorkshire Railway in 1880 transformed Hellifield by creating a busy rail junction. This led to a building boom for the many railway workers and their families. Much has been lost but the rail junction remains. Look for cast-iron wyverns (emblem of the Midland Railway) on the canopy at the "island" station, where once there was noise and bustle throughout the twenty-four hours. A new road links the A.65 with the station.

Knocker-up. When, before the Beeching era, Hellifield station throbbed with life, and the village was truly a railway community, the knocker-up made his doleful rounds with a rod long enough to enable him to rap on bedroom windows. He would shout "Double-head to Carlisle" or "Relief to Manchester." And the driver, the fire-man or the guide, the sleep mist still on his eyes, would respond with a tap on the inside of the bedroom window. The railwayman often had unsocial hours. Hellifield wives knew the heartache of keeping food warm for so long it became part of the cooker.

Jimmy Fishwick recalled for me when the words "...and lodge" at the end of the knocker-up's message meant the railwayman would spend a night away from home. To Jim Antell, the word "lodge" recalled accommodation in bunks at Dent. Brief interludes of sleep interspersed furious spells of work as the snow ploughs that were quartered at Hellifield were directed to clearing snow from blocked cuttings.

Alf Roberts used to say of the knocker-up: "It was a poor job for a lad, trailing about in all weathers."

Normally, an hour's grace was allowed from being knocked-up to getting to work. If two chaps were to be called at the same time, the knocker-up might have to walk from one end of the village to the other. The second man to be knocked-up would then be pushed for time

Jimmy Fishwick's hair stood on end early one day when, while going on his rounds as knocker-up, he became aware of a ghostly, silent figure walking beside him. Then he saw a third man, mounted on a bicycle. The walker was an entrant for the forthcoming Bradford to Morecambe walk who was limbering up before the great day.

Eventually, the knockers-up were knocked off. Nobody regretted the decision.

The Long Pull. In the days of steam traction, the storekeeper, Peter Crossley, normally a most conscientious man, had to resort to subterfuge over his oil returns. A driver who came for oil wanted the storeman to be generous and give him "the long pull." The quantity of oil in the tank rarely agreed with the figure in the book. Jimmy Fishwick recalled that when he started work, he was helping Peter, who one day asked him to get some firebricks, which were kept in "the back place."

When Jimmy asked how many firebricks to collect, he was told to fill a barrow. He duly delivered the bricks. Peter said: "Put them in the

Blue Billy," which was a quite large tank holding a grade of oil that was blueish in colour. An official was due to inspect the stores. As Jimmy placed firebricks in the tank, Peter took frequent dipstick readings until the level of oil accorded with the quantity on the books.

Passenger locomotives were allocated G oil, which was especially thick. It ran so slowly from a barrel into a bucket that Jimmy and others were inclined to leave the tap turned on while they did other jobs. It was not uncommon for the storeman to return and see G oil oozing under the door, the bucket having overflowed. Sand was quickly strewn on the floor to absorb the oil.

Talented. Nearly every Settle-Carlisle signalman had another job he could carry out while on duty. Percy Woodall, a signalman at Hellifield goods yard, was a cobbler. Jackie Sedgwick at Dent was a barber. In another box, the speciality was jam-making, using the signalbox stove. A third man "used to paint anything for anybody." A signalman with restless fingers might tinker about with bits of cars, such as carburettors, which he had taken to work with him.

At one box, during the Second World War, where the duty signalman was a kindly man who did not mind bending a few rules, several farm lads – "poor little lads, they were not right well fed" – arrived regularly with stolen poultry and any amount of eggs, which could be boiled in a kettle. They also brought potatoes to make chips. "We had some wonderful evening meals." When the relief signalman was due about 10 o'clock "them lads vanished into the mist."

Cattle Wagons. The first train that Richard Fawcett (Rabbity Dick) worked as a goods guard was the 9-15 out of Heysham and the first stop was Hellifield, to put off some Irish "beeasts" for Hellifield auction. On that line, there was an up-and-down gradient. "When the cattle reached Hellifield, they were usually train-sick."

Cattle that were reared on the almost treeless Outer Hebrides, and which outwintered on the gale-swept machair, were sold to Dales graziers, shipped to Oban and put on steam-hauled cattle wagons for delivery, journeys end being points along the Settle-Carlisle line. They emerged from the cattle vans "looking thin and brown, like kippers" but soon rallied through eating the lush grass of the Craven district.

William Foster and his son Eric, who farmed Little Newton, within sight of Hellifield station, visited Oban and the Isles for many years to buy cattle. Eric paid his first vists in 1930, when he was still at school. His last stock-buying trip into Scotland was in 1965. At Oban, the steam-driven *Princess Louise,* of 105 tons, owned privately, was employed on the cattle run. On one trip, the crossing the Minch took place in such wild weather that, back at home and at school, Eric found that for a day or two his stomach was still rolling with the sea.

As Eric unloaded his cattle from the railway cattle wagons at Hellifield and turned them into his big field to graze, he noticed time and time again that they went all round the field, as though to check on its size and shape, before going to the stream to drink and prepared to graze. The cattle dock at Hellifield station closed during the run-down of facilities. "It was a pity, for the railways had given us good service at a minimum cost."

Price of Tea. In 1947, Derek Soames was a junior porter at Hellifield, which then bustled with life. Some non-corridor trains stopped briefly for convenience (there were handy toilets). The porters modestly augmented their wages by conveying cups of tea from the tearoom to waiting passengers. The counter price for a cup of tea was $1\frac{1}{2}$d but a member of the staff obtained it for one penny, so each trip yielded a profit of halfpence.

Derek presented an old lady with her cup and the train pulled out before she had time to pay him. Three weeks later, Derek was summoned to the stationmaster's office and asked if he was the employee who three weeks before provided an old lady with a cup of tea for which he had not been paid. The stationmaster had received a letter from her enclosing a cheque for 1s.6d in payment. On this occasion, Derek's lapse was overlooked.

Settle Junction

This is the start of the Settle-Carlisle. The engineers had to have a smooth clearance of the summat at Aisgill, so the line has a ruling gradient of 1 in 100, with an initial long embankment. The so-called Long Drag is the 22 miles of almost continual ascent from Settle to Aisgill, with half a mile of level track at Helwith Bridge.

Steam and Diesel. A Carlisle driver who enjoyed the Settle Carlisle said it was a challenge. "For a steam special, we always got water at Long Preston. Then we got a good fire on and a good head of steam and caught the distant signal at Settle Junction. Normally, to be fair, it was always 'off' for us. If you started slipping in the first of two cuttings, you were struggling. I remember when we slipped in the second cutting, just short of Stainforth Tunnel. There was over an inch of slime from rotten leaves on the rail. In such conditions there was a diesel standing at Settle Junction in case you stuck. I contacted the signalman. The diesel came up behind us and coupled on. A friend of mine was sitting at Selside with his camera set at a certain speed for the best kind of photograph. With the diesel at our back, we were doing sixty miles an hour."

Fiery Wheels. In the days of loose-coupled wagons, the guard of a freight train was expected to be a skilled operator of the handbrake that was a prominent feature of his van. To work it properly, he must know the gradients. One of the finest places to observe the guard's display of "fireworks" as the brake clenched the wheels at night, throwing out lots of sparks, was from a train that stood at the signal on the Morecambe line, awaiting clearance from the box at Settle Junction. On the downward gradient, the wheels glowed like Catherine wheels. When Derek Soames began work at the Settle Junction box, in 1973, people who had seen the Catherine wheel effect rang in to say there was a train on fire.

Cobs of Coal. The signal box was erected in 1913 and is therefore a genuine Midland Railway structure, though the frame was replaced in 1959. In the steam days, a signalman who was running short of coal could rely on the driver of a locomotive tossing off a few big cobs. A fireman did not like the effort of breaking up a really big cob, so he contrived to have it on the footplate, ready for tipping off. It was usually good Yorkshire coal. If you hit it with a hammer, it broke into slabs. It was just like "riving" slate. When a signalman put it on the fire, it crackled.

A Nomadic Crane. In 1979, when a northbound freight was derailed at Settle Junction, the locomotive remained on the rails but over 40 wagons, many of them containing china clay, formed a heap of wreckage so high that looking from the signal box the wrecked wagons blocked a view of the over-bridge to the north. Control sent from Carlisle one of the last remaining steam cranes, which picked up wrecked wagons and deposited them on low-loaders or on the bank sides. When no more could be recovered from this direction, the huge crane was taken back to Carlisle, down the West Coast line and back up through Arkholme to attack the debris from another angle. Many years after the derailment, traces of the china clay are to be found at Settle Junction.

Second in Command. Derek had a companion in the Settle Junction signal box – his dog Muttley, who died aged 14 and was buried in the banking behind the box, with a wooden cross (made of timber from a redundant signal post) to mark the spot. If for any reason Derek had to go outside the box, he could hear little else but road traffic. If a bell or a telephone rang in the box, Muttley gave a short bark and looked round, as much as to say: "Come on – there's a bell ringing."

Settle

The station is of the large Midland type, as allocated to market towns along the course of the line. The buildings were well constructed of stone from the Bradford area. Notice the attractive "finishing touches," such as in the fretted bargeboards. Settle had a goods shed, an extensive goods yard. Coal from the deep beds of the South Yorkshire coalfield arrived at a siding allocated to this traffic. Many of the trucks seen in North Ribblesdale bore the name of a local quarry-owner, John Delaney, the name being presented in large white letters. Samuel Owen Leadbeater, who was a permanent way inspector from just north of Skipton to Garsdale, residing at No. 1 Goldielands, Settle, from 1904 until 1915, received £2 a week. He was one who agitated for better conditions for the railway workers. The signal box that presided over the sidings has been restored by the Friends of the Settle-Carlisle Line.

A Lovely Little Box. If you worked in a box like Settle all your life, as did Albert Carter, you were in clover. Richard Fawcett recalled of the early 1940s: "When I was getting a little wage as a platelayer, the Settle signalman was a rich man, earning £2.10s a week. If you had Sunday work it brought you up to £3.15s a week. You were a gentleman. I flogged away until I got into a box." The Settle box was busy. "There would be a train each road every twenty minutes. That meant a train

every ten minutes. Then you had one or two different shunts. There was a full-time shunter at the station."

Ups and Downs. During the Second World War, a guard on a freight train that left Hellifield for Carlisle, was applying the brake when the need had not arisen. The footplate crew quickly deduced this from the sluggish nature of the train. They made a shortage of water the excuse for stopping at Settle station. The fireman hurried back to the van, where he confronted the guard. He confessed that none of his training as a guard on the Plain of York had prepared him for the ups and downs of the Settle-Carlisle. When in doubt, he was dropping some ball-bearings on the floor and seeing in which direction they ran.

The Old Box. In February, 1997, Railtrack allowed the Friends to strip the interior fittings from the Victorian signal box so that this structure might be lifted from the lineside and given a new position nearer the station. During a brief summer night, the box was lifted by crane on to rail bogies, trundled along the line, then lifted again and placed in its new situation. The box has been virtually rebuilt by voluntary labour and in its restored state has once again assumed the Midland colours of maroon and cream. The signal levers were intact but the block instruments and other equipment had been removed by British Rail. The volunteers visited the Midland Railway Centre at Butterley, Derbyshire and, as recounted by Glyn Hague, "we were taken into the Signal and Telegraph Stores, which really are like an Aladdin's cave where we were able to select as required. We came home with two car boots well filled with signal box parts." The signal outside the box is an old distant signal from Blea Moor.

Stainforth

This is where the the line crosses a geological fault. A tunnel was driven beneath the grounds of Taitlands, a private house that for long has been a youth hostel. The Midland company paid for the family to live elsewhere to avoid the disturbance while the tunnel was being driven.

Hoffman's Kiln. Between Langcliffe and Stainforth lay Craven Quarry, with its notable kiln, devised for the continuous burning of limestone and named after its German inventor. A chimney some 200ft high rose from the centre of the long structure. Jimmy Fishwick, a driver from Hellifield, had problems with his fireman on the Drag. The fire was too low for the task immediately ahead. He summoned his fireman across the footplate and pointed to the top of the chimney at the Hoffman kiln, observing: "In the next few miles, the track is going to reach the height of that chimney. The fireman gawped, then was galvanised into activity. Coal seem to fly on to the fire!"

Lucky Escapes. The signal box that stood at Stainforth controlled busy sidings that were connected with the Hoffman. Coal for the kiln arrived by rail and the burnt lime went out by the same means. The signal box was on the outside of a curve down which trains sometimes travelled much faster than intended. Richard Fawcett worked here at a time when the quarry had a dozen horses to haul trucks in the quarry. "It was a simple, easy box. I was always frightened of the accident that eventually did happen. There was a lot of cant on the rails. I've known me go out of the box at Stainforth, I was that scared that one day a train would leave the tracks and take the front out."

The first box was demolished by a wagonload of sheet steel that sliced through it, narrowly missing the signalman on duty. The second box was wrecked by a train of runaway tanker wagons. The signalman lost his bike, which he stabled within the box at ground level. There was talk of fitting an ejector seat!

Shortage of Coal. On the first occasion when there was a mishap at Stainforth, and huge pieces of steel were tipped down a banking to clear the line, a steam-crane was sent from Carlisle on the Saturday night, following the last "Pancras" out, to attend to the displaced steel, each piece resembling a giant soup dish. No one who helped remove them knew what they were intended to do.

The fireman on a locomotive, Ivatt class, sent out from Carlisle on the Sunday morning to relieve the crane recalls: "That class of engine, which was brought out in 1947, had a very small tender. Away we went. It poured down all the time we were there. When it was coming-home time, I got into the tender and shovelled the coal forward. There were about two or three hundredweight in the bottom. My mate said: 'We'll couple up to the crane'. I said: 'We haven't much coal. Do you think we should go to Hellifield?' He growled: 'No – we'll be all right'.

"We didn't get to Ribblehead. We run out of coal. The crane was stuck. Dead duck. They had to send to Carlisle for another engine. It was a serious business. The crane could have been sent for anytime. There was a bit of a stink about it at Carlisle. 'We'd booked on at eleven o' clock on the Sunday morning and we didn't get back into Kingmoor until five on the Monday morning. My mate had gone to bed. The boss said: 'Send for him. Wake him up. Get him down here!' The driver nearly got the sack for it."

Helwith Bridge

The signal box served the quarries and was run at one time by Richard (Dick) Clarke, who cycled from Clapham to perform his duties. Dick, who wore flannel next to his skin the year through, often had a face as red as a turkey-cock after his cycling exertions. It was a time when an incline railway from the limestone belt atop Moughton Fell was operated by gravity-laden trucks coming down providing the power via an endless rope for empties that were going up. It was all handwork. Teams of men shovelled road chippings into the railway wagons drawn up in the sidings.

Horton-in-Ribblesdale

Horton station is a splendid vantage point for Penyghent, "hill of the winds," if the weather is clear! The hill, which has the necessary 2,000ft-plus for mountainhood, resembles a crouching lion. West of the railway is Beecroft Quarry, developed by the aforementioned John Delaney, who built a house at Settle but arranged for a large kit of spring water from his quarry to be delivered by rail and used in his household. He did not like to drink Settle tap water.

Smoked Railwaymen. Many moons ago, a workman's coach was left in a siding at Horton-in-Ribblesdale. It was a standard coach, though stripped of its furnishings to provide space for benches and cooking facilities. Two stoves were used for heating and one for cooking, which was a task given to the nipper

– the term for a lad who had just joined the gang or an old man who was due for retirement. The Appleby gang were sheltering in the coach as rain fell as though from a celestial hosepipe.

A workman at the signal box placed flat stones on the chimneys of the coach. For about half an hour, there was no response. The anxious signalman said the man must have suffocated them. Cautiously opening the door, the workman saw men playing cards. Another man was lying down. A third poured paraffin on to the stove, which appeared to be blocked! The upper part of the coach was a thick mass of smoke that came down to within a foot or so of the men and threatened to overwhelm them. When the practical joker saw the Appleby gang evacuate the coach, he went to recover the stone and was seen by the nipper. Henceforth, he dare not even approach the Appleby Gang for fear of retribution.

Lots of Shunts. Though it is a small station, Horton-in-Ribblesdale handled a vast amount of freight, mainly lime from Beecroft Quarry,

the entrance by rail being a trailing connection at the east end of the "down" platform. A goods guard who worked the Settle-Carlisle in the late 1930s recalls: "Shunts? We'd lots o' shunts. Up at Horton, you'd shunt the station yard. Carter Metcalfe was the shunter here and he told us precisely where he wanted everything. He'd say: 'I want 15 empties shoved up into t'quarry'."

Empty wagons needed at the extensive works had to be rushed through points, around a bend and up a sharp incline. It was a spectacular operation when a lime train was involved. A locomotive hauled forty or fifty empty wagons beyond the starting signal prior to

Continued on page 49

Bill Sharpe, the last stationmaster at Ribblehead, photographed on the platform with his son, Geoffrey, who was serving as a porter. In Bill's day, Ribblehead was also a weather station. *(Photo: W R Mitchell).*

Above: A light engine of the type used in the Ribblesdale quarries. *(Author's collection).*
Below: Mrs Taylor, wife of Jim Taylor, tends her husband's garden on the up-platform of Settle Station. *(Photo: W R Mitchell).*

A mounted farmer out "kenning" sheep on Blea Moor is pictured beside the water-crane, long since removed. *(Photo: W R Mitchell).*

45596 "Bahamas" climbs through Mallerstang, the valley that is the "cradle" of the River Eden. *(Photo: Peter Fox).*

Above: A "steam special," 46229, has a stop for water at Garsdale.
Below: A northbound pick-up in the siding at Aisgill. *(Photos: W R Mitchell).*

Above: Settle-Carlisle country. Penyghent is seen beyond the Ribble near Helwith Bridge. The windmill was long since removed. *Below:* A section of a redundant signal box used as a greenhouse at Long Marton. *(Author's collection).*

Snow-blocked cutting, Dent, in the winter of 1963. The photographs were taken by an engine driver, Isaac Hailwood, of Hellifield.

Above: Signal box near the level crossing at Culgaith, in the Eden Valley.
(Photo: W R Mitchell). Below: A Cumbrian Mountain Express heads south from
Mallerstang. *(Photo: Peter Fox).*

reversing them up the bank. Jim Taylor, stationmaster for several years, recalled having to make sure that the points were set right.

The empties went up the front road, there being another set of points sending them round the corner rather than into the stop-blocks. The shunter, having gone to the quarry office to ensure their points were correctly set, gave Jim the tip. He relayed it to the driver and, as soon as he received it, and to use Jim's expression, it was "wham – clank, clank, clank, zzzzz!!" as the shunting took place.

If the train stuck, it would be taken further up the main line and another attempt made. One set of points caused innumerable derailments over the years. In this case, blocks were used to get the trucks back on the track. In extreme conditions, the Hellifield steam crane was summoned.

Toasted Teacake. It was Jim Taylor who set up the Legend of the Toasted Teacake. When trains were steam-hauled, they may have to stop at Horton to await clearance of the track ahead. The delay might be caused by an inexperienced fireman, by bad coal or by an engine pulling badly. In those days, expresses would be operating within minutes of each other, with one standing on block behind another. Jim used to go to the Carlisle side in case someone wanted to get out when the train stopped. "It doesn't matter where a train stops, someone always wants to be out."

He was on the platform when a train drew in and came to a halt, waiting for the "road." There was invariably a dining car (later reduced to a buffet car) and, as usual, one of the staff on board the train asked the reason for the unexpected stop. Jim would tell them the reason for the delay and assure them they would be on their way in a few minutes. He added: "By the way, you haven't kept up the old custom." "What's that?"

Jim continued: "Didn't you know that whenever you stop at Horton-in-Ribblesdale you must always see that the Stationmaster, who is usually on the platform, is presented with a toasted teacake. "Is that reight?" the startled railman would ask, just before he darted off to get a toasted teacake on a plate. He must have spread the news round by bush-telegraph. From that day, Jim had a toasted teacake handed out with due ceremony as he stood on the platform.

A Large Order. When a hiker's train was de-railed at Appleby, and both up and down tracks were blocked, Jim had two hundred people waiting on Horton station for that train, which would take them back to Leeds. Jim rang across to Joe Barker, of Beecroft Farm, and mentioned he had two hundred thirsty and hungry folk to deal with. "Get your wife to make us a brew up of good strong coffee and we'll do the same here – and keep it going." The hikers were provided with food and drink.

A Matter of Compensation. One of Jim Taylor's minor jobs as Stationmaster was to meet any farmer who had put in a claim for the loss of a sheep, which coincidentally was always the best animal in the flock. (A hill sheep would jump a lineside wall to get an early bite of grass in springtime). Where injury or death occurred, Jim must visit the farmer and arrange an amicable settlement.

The conversation would go as follows: "Ay, hello Mr Taylor. Come on in. Noo then, what can I do for thee? Wilt hev a drink?" Jim would state his business – that he had arrived about the ewe that was killed on the railway track. The farmer would reflect on this. "Oh, aye, eee – by gow, I were sad aboot that. Aye." The farmer would utter a deep sigh and continue: "She were carrying two lambs an' all. I cut her oppen...Ay, it were a pity, that. Aye." Jim would say: "Well, we propose to give you two pounds ten for her." "What!" the farmer would screech, hurt beyond measure. The settlement was usually about three pounds.

Selside

The nameboard SELSIDE on a roadside building originally adorned a local signal box, of basic design, that was intended to split up the long section of track between Horton and Ribblehead. (The restored signal box is now on view at Carnforth). The last man to work this box was Richard Fawcett.

Brought to a Halt. Two Appleby men who attended an emergency call to Selside were faced with the prospect of having to walk down to Horton to catch a train home. They were refused permission to wave down a goods train and so, just round the nearest bend from the man in authority, they oiled the rails and then sat back. Before long a goods train arrived. While it was slithering on the oily stretch, the two men boarded the guards van.

Women in Charge. During the 1939-45 war, Selside was the only main line signal box that was operated round the clock by signalwomen. There was no cross-over road – "just two levers one way and two levers t'other way." Selside, by evening out the length of the sections, saved

a lot of delays, especially in bad weather. Jimmy Fishwick, who became a driver, recalled that when a northbound train was kept standing at the signal for a considerable period, the driver, a Leeds-based man, eventually mounted the steps of the box and, with the signal in mind, said: "Come on – get 'em, off!" The lady on duty slapped his face and reported him to Control for insolence.

Big John. George Horner had a funny experience when his duties were centred on Selside signal box. His car was off the road for a while in winter. He walked to the box from his home at Horton-in-Ribblesdale. "It had come a fair bit of snow during the night. I was on early turn, beginning at six o'clock. I went down Lambert's Yard, heading for the stile on the path leading to t'box. It was dark apart from t'signal box light. I could see this fellow walking ahead of me. I thought it was a local botanist, who was out and about at all daylight hours."

George was surprised when, instead of going up to the box, this figure went up the bank by the lamp-hut and across the tracks. "I thought no more about it until all of a sudden I stopped in my tracks and my hair stood on end. Ahead of me, there wasn't a footmark to be seen on the newly-fallen snow." George entered the box. He must have been looking white for the signalman he was relieving said: "Tha looks as if tha's sin a ghost." George told his story. The signalman knew the ghost and had a name for him. It was Big John. "He's been around a bit," he added, unemotionally.

Salt Lake

Salt Lake Cottages are incongruous. It is as though a segment of Coronation Street had strayed from Salford to this remote spot with its backdrop of Whernside. The terrace, which has a vaguely gothic style, is faced with dressed stone. The chimneys are prominent. Three double-sided projecting porches give the row a further touch of distinction.

Snowbound. In 1947, when the railway was blocked by snow at the cutting between Ribblehead Viaduct and Blea Moor, the inhabitants of Salt Lake Cottages were cut off for eight weeks by road but had a rail link with Settle. Selected freight trains stopped to off-load fuel and other necessities. It would be sunny during the day. "Then after five o'clock t'wind would get up and blow the snow back into the areas you'd cleared."

The platelayers made a snow platform at Salt Lake and local folk walked across the snow directly into the train. A loco driver shouted to Mrs Towler: "Do you want some black snow?" She had no idea what he was talking about, but accepted the offer. He asked her to bring him a sack, which he half-filled with coal from the tender. The Towlers had just had a pig killed. They exchanged bacon for coal.

Having worked for twelve hours in gruelling conditions, Jack Towler returned to his Salt Lake Cottage home and removed his overcoat with difficulty. It was so frosted it stood up on its own accord. "There was no easy work in them days." Afterwards he was off work for some weeks with frost-bitten nose and ears.

The most astonishing bid to clear snow from the line occurred in March, 1947. It was a jet-powered snow plough. Two jet engines were mounted on a flat wagon, it being reasoned that the heat they generated would melt the snow, which it did, though what resulted was a casing of ice, making matters worse. Jack Towler describes what happened: "This fire-blower came on Saturday morning and as per usual when they got it fixed up it wouldn't go. They had to send for someone to fix it up and when they got set off and made arrangements for all points to be clipped at Blea Moor for it to go through – it was going to go straight through to Dent – it didn't go from 'ere to that couch [a few feet]. All it did was blow a bit o' snow out of t'bottom there and blow t'ballast out onto t'moor. When it finished, t'place where it were working were all ice."

Foggy Weather. When Jack Towler was married in 1932, he had just returned from his honeymoon to a home at one of the railway cottages at Salt Lake when he was called out at night to go fogging. In foggy weather, when the loco drivers had no clear view of the signals, men were stationed on either side of the viaduct and at Salt Lake. "Each of us had a flag and a hand lamp that showed red or green. We also had some detonators. If the signal was at danger, we'd put a detonator on the line. A train that cracked a detonator was also shown a red flag as he passed us."

Toasted Kippers. Every Thursday, Alf Flack, of Salt Lake, arrived at Ribblehead station with a supply of big Scotch kippers. Jack Towler recalled that "we'd toast 'em in front of t'fire for our dinner." Living in a cottage at Salt Lake was George Cockles, Kate Flack and Alf, her son. The men called them, respectively, "he say," "she say" and "I say." That was how they used to talk.

Ribblehead

Ribblehead, an area where several valleys meet, experiences strong westerly gales that send the sheep scurrying for shelter. The most prominent feature after Whernside is the railway viaduct, 440 yards long and with a maximum height of just over 100 ft. There are 24 arches.

Wind in the Wagons. Richard Fawcett could hark back to a time when "there were whole trains made up of cattle wagons... If it was blowing owt like at Ribblehead, and you had a lot of empty cattle wagons, you were lucky to get across. About t'only train that really stuck on the viaduct were cattle wagons. T'owd engine, by t'time it got there, was getting tired. You can imagine a horse doing t'same. When it wanted most of its breath, it'd lost it. On top of that, a wind in the wagons acted like a brake."

In Time of War. During the 1939-45 war, there were "any amount of red warnings and bits o' frights and listening to planes droning over. Some of t'lads would say – 'that's one of ours'. Another would say – 'that's a bloody Jerry'. They reckoned to be able to tell the difference from the pitch of the engine. A sort of drone."

No bombs fell at Ribblehead but the sound of explosions were heard. The Towlers had gone to bed at their cottage at Salt Lake when, about 10p.m., which was "the time the German planes went to Belfast," they heard a plane approaching. "It wasn't three minutes before that plane was back again; it had dropped bombs at Cloughton brickworks. We heard the bang."

Ganger Jack Towler and his men were returning from working at Blea Moor at 5p.m. one misty wartime day. "We got as far as Ribblehead and heard a big aeroplane coming over, droning away. I says: 'He'll have to look out, the way he's going'. We didn't get much further when there was such a bang. A Lancaster bomber had crashed into Whernside." Next morning, Jack looked through the staircase window at Salt Lake and saw the remains of the huge plane. The five crew members perished; their bodies were reverently carried to Winterscales Farm and placed in the sitting room until they were claimed by the RAF. For years afterwards, on a sunny day, the Salt Lakers looked high on Whernside to see the sparkle from a piece of aircraft left embedded in the ground.

The Intruder. At Salt Lake, one Monday, as a housewife was "getting the clothes ready in the wash-house," she glanced across the yard to see a cow entering her home. "I'd left t'back gate open. A farm man was driving the cows up the back lane into the field above. One of the cows had broken away. I screamed. The farm man arrived, but not afore the cow had gone through into my sitting room and had come out again. He said it was a wonder it had not tried to jump through the window. I said it was a wonder it had not done anything on the floor. He'd have had to clean it up!"

Time for Worship. When Joe Shepherd was the stationmaster at Ribblehead, permission was obtained to hold services in the waiting room where, just after the construction period of the 1870s, the spirit of the old Batty Green mission persisted. The Shepherds and the Towlers had decided to get the children together on one Sunday afternoon a month, and at its peak this unusual dalehead place of worship had an attendance of over 35 children. Among the worshippers were the Coates family from the Station Inn, the Duttons from Winterscales and the Masons of Lodge Hall.

The Vicar of Ingleton, the Rev H J Croft, had agreed to take the service and to bring hymn books. He used as a rostrum the short-flat-topped barrier that stood near the window of the ticket office. Mrs Whinray did her best to play the harmonium. Students from Methodism's Cliffe College, in Derbyshire, who visited the district, added gusto to some of the services with their lively singing. George Horner recalls that when the Rev Croft was late, he reckoned it was time to lend a hand. George "got up to t'lectern and said: 'Let us praise God and sing Rule 55'." As he spoke the words, the Vicar and George's mother and father walked into the waiting room. His parents were not amused.

Jolly Dances. Whist drives and dances were held at the station. Dancing took place in the ladies room, which had a wooden floor. The general waiting room, which was stone-flagged, was t'supper room. George Horner had an old HMV wind-up gramophone that provided music for dancing. "We had Victor Sylvester and Harry Davidson – only the best!" The District Operating Superintendent and his wife turned up now and again. He said that a dance at Ribblehead provided him with one of the best nights of entertainment he'd had in his life. That worthy added: "They are jolly do's. By all means carry on organising them."

Ribblehead Viaduct

The viaducts of the Settle-Carlisle provide the greatest visual appeal, none more so than Blea Moor (originally called Batty Moss viaduct) which has 24 arches and a length of l,328ft. The viaduct is buttressed by imposing embankments. It was constructed in sections, from north to south.

A Bit of a Blow. When a gale was rampaging through the district, platelayers were called out. Freight trains with sheeted wagons were stopped in the sidings at Blea Moor and the sheets tightened so that in their passage across the exposed viaduct they would not be blown away, to become a windfall in a literal sense for local farmers. (Every farmer had a railway wagon sheet). Some windborne sheets travelled like parachutes for up to half a mile.

"There'll still be bits o' wagon sheet on yon moorland." A store was maintained at Blea Moor. It contained new wagon sheets to replace those that had been lost.

A Stray Rope. George Cockles, who hailed from Newmarket, was in charge of the gang of five when Jack Towler joined it in 1924. George told some fanciful tales, such as the time when a goods train crossing the viaduct had a wagon with a sheet hanging. A rope caught George around the neck, but he had the presence of mind to put his hand in his pocket, while running alongside the train, to get out his knife and cut the rope.

Perhaps it was Cockles who first told the daft story of a man who was crossing Ribblehead viaduct when a wind blew the cap off his head, took it under an arch and up the other side, dropping it back on his head – with the neb at the back instead of at the front. (Such a cross-wind was carried by the parapet high above a man's head). Jack said: "You could feel t'viaduct tremblin' in certain places when trains were coming over. Frost was inclined to lift t'lines up, especially at Settle end. The situation was somewhat better than Arten Gill, where "we'd to put a caution on trains."

In 1947, prisoners of war were brought up in ballast trains to clear snow from Ribblehead station and dump it over the parapets of the viaduct. Jack Towler remembered one lot of prisoners who refused to leave the warm train to clear snow. "When eventually the inspector got them out and the wagons were filled and moved to the viaduct, the prisoners refused to empty them. That inspector was a very religious man. They 'turned him'. I'd never heard a man swear as much in all my life! He said: 'If my wife could hear me now, she'd drop down dead'."

Look, Duck and Vanish. The Home Guard (originally the LDV, which locals nicknamed Look, Duck and Vanish) paid special attention to the viaduct, which they regularly patrolled from sentry boxes set at either end. Little heed was paid to possible Fifth Column activity at ground level, about 100 feet below the trackbed. Elsewhere, "you'd see them skulking behind walls. It was laughable." The men mustered in the waiting room at Ribblehead station, where one man, demonstrating to a friend that there was no bullet "in the spout," pointed his rifle upwards, pulled the trigger and sent a bullet through the ceiling and slates into the wide blue yonder.

A Mysterious Coffin. When Ribblehead viaduct was being restored, a "shanty town" of portable cabins and a portable loo appeared almost in the shadow of the huge structure. The Wigan man who was in charge of the scaffolding team allowed me to see inside their quarters, which were luxurious compared with the standards of the 1870s when Ribblehead viaduct was under construction. Then the most favoured workers occupied plain wooden huts with stoves. The scaffolding team had one man more than planned. A worker was left without a bed. He used his special skills and made one – from scaffolding and planks.

The restored viaduct had become, slyly, the last resting place of a number of railway fanatics. Their friends left urns with their ashes beside the viaduct and putting them in the structure was, unofficially, one way to dispose of them. Tony Freschini, who was the resident engineer at Ribblehead during its major restoration, and who certainly did not condone the illicit interments, was working in his office at the base of the viaduct on a wild January day when one of the workmen reported seeing a coffin on the viaduct.

Tony and three members of his staff climbed up to the viaduct and had a distant view of "something" that was propped against a parapet. As they neared it, the object was undoubtedly a coffin, from which protruded an arm. A silver plate on the outside of the coffee was inscribed with the word "Walter." The arm was made of rubber. Grasping the lid, which was loose, Tony threw it back with a scream that made his companions flee in terror. The coffin was empty. It was, as someone remarked, 'armless.

Blea Moor

At the southern edge of the moor stood an isolated cluster of buildings, including signal box (originally by the "down" line), water tower and a few cottages for workmen and their families. Letters for the Blea Moor community were delivered by the Chapel-le-Dale postman, who operated on foot. Groceries were transported to Blea Moor by the stopping freight train. In the 1940s, sidings were replaced by two passing loops that "caused a lot o' bother, wi' derailments and wagins brekking loose and running away."

"Parky" Weather. George Horner was at Blea Moor box when the new signalman's inspector called and remarked on the grand setting of the box. "You can see for miles," he added. George observed that conditions were not quite as good when snowflakes were flying. Three years or so later, in 1963, during a grim spell of weather, the inspector returned – in charge of the snowplough.

George was at the box at Horton, on the low side of which the snow had formed a large drift. The plough eventually made it to Blea Moor. On the return, it stopped at Horton. As the inspector, who by now resembled the Abominable Snowman, came up the steps of the box, George gently reminded him of what he had said about the grand views. He did at least see the humour of the situation.

At the Blea Moor signal box, paraffin lamps were used as lighting. Paraffin was delivered by rail in large drums. "At one time you had a lile bit of a light over t'book. Boss said that if there were too much leet in t'box you couldn't see what was going on outside. Main thing you saw outside on a really dark night was a hot axle box." A signalman usually had a singing kettle on the stove. Some rudimentary cooking was undertaken. One chap, breaking open an egg, and dropping the contents on to the top of the stove, said he was roasting it.

Shortest Way. William Davison, who was a member of the Blea Moor maintenance gang for 13 years, and lived with his family at one of the local cottages, was a Methodist local preacher with a bike. If he had a Sunday appointment, he would carry his bike across Ribblehead viaduct to reach the nearest road. When planned to preach at Dent, he invariably carried his bike through Blea Moor Tunnel. He knew the times of the trains and "there was not much traffic on a Sunday."

The Runaway. A monkey-muck [iron ore] train ran backwards from Blea Moor – all the way to Long Preston. It was during the Second World War and the loop was full at Blea Moor. The signalman had nothing on the "up" road but had expresses on the "down." He backed the monkey-muck train across the tracks and a sudden jerk broke the coupling behind the engine. As the trucks started running away, the guard leapt off, helplessly watching as the guards van and eighteen or twenty wagons went off as steady as an express.

At Stainforth, the signalman left the box, expecting a collision. Emergency signals were set at other boxes. The biggest shock was to a group of platelayers who had the sudden appearance of wagons led by a guard van but no engine. The runaways came to a halt, as related, at Long Preston.

Woolly Trespassers. Sheep that should have been content with moorland fare strayed on to the railway, especially in early spring, looking for toothsome bites. Some were knocked down and killed but mostly the sheep that were habitually on the railway adjusted themselves to the traffic and were nonchalent at the approach of a train. Some sheep were "lambed at t'railway side" and regarded it as home.

At Blea Moor, a tup – known to George Horner as t'owd devil – gave way before an irate platelayer but soon afterwards was back, stamping its forefeet at him. A ewe that lay in the four-foot, chewing her cud, alarmed an inspector visiting the Blea Moor signal box and George was instructed to remove her. He said: "Let her stop theer." The inspector said she would be run over by a train. George replied: "That's her b— look out." The night express was offered and accepted. The inspector was keeping his eye on the sheep.

"In a bit there was a rumbling and this big yellow nose on t'express came under t'bridge. The sheep was still there. The inspector said: 'I can't watch this'. In the end he could not resist looking. He saw the old sheep get up, stretch and walk out of the way. The express passed her at sixty miles an hour. When it had gone, the sheep returned to the four-foot and lay down again."

Another inspector, who was travelling on the footplate of a train, saw – when the train emerged from the south portal of Blea Moor tunnel – there were several sheep on the track. The inspector said: "I suppose you'll stop at the box and report them." Said the driver: "Will I heck. They're allus there." More sheep were seen just north of Selside. The driver stopped at the box to report them, saying to the inspector: "Them at Blea Moor were at home. These are fresh 'uns. They don't know their way about."

George told a relief stationmaster that story when he came up to Blea Moor. "I said the sheep knew 'trains as well as we did. It was only when they were heavy wi' lamb they might mis-judge the situation and get dabbed." The relief stationmaster inquired what would happen if there were specials. George said: "It would be hard luck." When the next batch of special traffic notices arrived, there were some for plate-layers, some for signalmen and some headed BLEA MOOR SHEEP. The stationmaster had a sense of humour.

The Lost Shirt. One hot summer's day, George Horner was on duty at

Blea Moor box when men were re-laying in the cutting leading to the tunnel. Conditions in the cutting were uncomfortably hot and they had taken off their shirts. One chap hung his shirt on a willow bush growing at the line-side. "T'express was due.

I pegged her through. The look-out man blew his horn and the gang stood back to let her go. When the express passed me, I could see a shirt flapping about in the motion of the engine. I rang my mate at the next box to advise him about it. I had looked hard but couldn't see a man in the shirt.

When the gang finished work and were walking by the box, all but one was wearing a shirt. I said to this chap: 'What's happened to thi shirt?' He said the blooming express had githered it up off the willow bush I'd hung it on. What should he tell the missus? George suggested he tell her what had happened. Quick as a flash, he replied: 'And would *your* missus believe a story like that'?"

Taken Short. The toilet at Blea Moor signal box was an Elsan chemical toilet, in "a lile shack" at the top of the steps. A signalman who was a keen pipe-smoker settled himself on the toilet, struck a match, kindled the tobacco in his pipe – then dropped what he thought was a spent match between his legs into the toilet. Shortly afterwards, the temperature rose alarmingly as the match, having ignited the chemicals, started a fire and threatened to grill him.

Beside the Line. Nancy Edmondson, who spent her young days at one of the remote railway houses on Blea Moor, recalls that mother shopped at Settle on Tuesday. Her transport was the "pick up" slow train which theoretically dealt with goods. It was caught at Ribblehead and was known to stop at Blea Moor if her lineside figure was noticed. Bulk supplies were delivered monthly by rail from Settle.

On the wedding day for her sister Edith, the bridal transport was a Midland 4F that was brought to an unscheduled stop at the signals. Edith, hair still in curlers and wedding dress over one arm, boarded the train, which stopped for her at Ribblehead. She changed into her finery at the Station Inn and the wedding ceremony took place at St Leonard's Church, in Chapel-le-Dale.

Nancy's sister, Margaret, went into labour early, so her signalman husband's colleague stopped the up Thames-Clyde express. When getting her into a carriage, the guide pulled, her father shoved and several passengers gave assistance. An ambulance met the train at Settle. In due course, a son was delivered at the Cawder Ghyll maternity hospital in Skipton.

Grandstand View. Nancy Edmondson's most memorable day was April 18, 1952. She was aged thirteen and on a balmy spring day was sunbathing on the roof of the pig sty in the corner of the family garden, which adjoined the railway. Nancy heard an express approaching. There followed an almighty crash. As she sat up, the second of two locomotives toppled on to its side, followed by three of the carriages. Steam rose from the wreck.

Nancy and her mother dashed to the wreckage as the signalman, the only other person within a mile of the accident, summoned help. A carry-cot that had been propelled through a broken window contained a baby who, astonishingly, survived without injury. The living room of the Edmondson home became a casualty clearing station. The spot was so remote from a road it was a long time before the rescue service arrived. Meanwhile, most of the passengers were sunbathing on the embankment. The rescuers, seeing a line of reclining bodies, feared a high death toll – then laughed with relief. (Nancy was presented with a watch by the Railways Board. She still has the watch – and it still keeps good time).

Blea Moor Tunnel

Anyone who travels northwards through Blea Moor tunnel (2,629 yards)
passes from the county of North Yorkshire into Cumbria. The Tunnel reaches
a maximum depth of 500 feet below the moor. Three of the construction shafts
were retained to provide ventilation. A man named Thompson was being
lowered by winch down a shaft to inspect it when "two gormless fellows who
were in charge of the winch were gabbling to each other, let go – and he fell and
broke both legs."

Brickies at Work. In about 1930, extensive repairs were needed to the
brickwork in Blea Moor Tunnel. Work was coming to an end, after fifteen years, of the re-lining of the two-mile long Morley Tunnel, near

Leeds. The men were regarded as "temporary" and when the Morley project was completed they were sacked and some were offered a job at Blea Moor, with the chance of residing in one of the nearby moorland cottages. Those who accepted worked a 47-hour week, from 6a.m. to 6p.m., less an hour for meals. They did this from Monday to Friday, by which time they had completed 44 hours. They had three hours left to do, and then (somehow) made their way back to Morley for the week-end, returning on Monday. The Blea Moor job extended over several years.

Above the Snowline. When word reached the outer world that the Settle-Carlisle was blocked with snow, two men were despatched from Lancaster to investigate. It was raining heavily in the city. As they headed for the hills, a snowline became visible, but there was green grass around them. They had a struggle in snow on the last stretch to Denthead.

Scrambling up the bank on to the viaduct, they saw smoke emerging from the big cabin at the north end of Blea Moor Tunnel. Old Joss appeared to view. He was a strange fellow, massive, clad in a jacket and waistcoat, with the buttons sewn on with different coloured wools, and coarse trousers. He had a cap with a hole in it. A great tuft of hair was sticking out of the top.

Joss inquired: "What's thoo doing 'ere?" One of the visitors said: "We'd heard there was a block and you were in a bit of bother." "Nay, lad," said Joss, in some amusement. "See yon hole [Blea Moor tunnel mouth]. I'll start to worry when I can't see any hole in there." The visitors realised their presence was not required.

Filthy Job. A member of the Tunnel Gang in the 1930s said: "Going in for the first time was a weird experience. It was half full of smoke, dead silent except for the occasional dripping of water and everything stank of sulphur. When a train entered Blea Moor tunnel, you could feel t'vibration and air pressure. The smoke used to be pushed back'ards and forrards by trains, then puffed out at t'top. On a still day, with no draught, you could hardly stir. We thought nothing of it.

When we emerged we were black as t'ace o'spades."

Smoky Mountain. The workers in Blea Moor Tunnel needed patience – and good lungs. The tunnel might be full of locomotive smoke or draped with icicles. The crew of the first train through after a hard night heard the crack of breaking ice as their engine came into contact. "It wasn't so bad unless you'd two or three double-heads through. Then it was a bit choky, but never so bad as in some other tunnels I knew." It was not unknown for a gang to enter the tunnel only to have a lazy day because of dense smoke. In the days of "duck lamps," the old men knew when a train was entering the tunnel by the state of the flame. "It used to suck the flame towards it."

In Devilish Mood. Harry Cox, labouring in Blea Moor tunnel just before the First World War, was provided with a white blanket coat by the company. (The coat did not stay white for long). A tunnel worker also had thigh-length leggings. The men were accustomed to walking through the tunnel in darkness, using the four-foot. They would tap a rail with a stick to maintain the right course. At other times, naptha lamps were used. "They smoked as they burnt." If a man felt a little devilish, he would "accidentally" knock a lamp over, causing a spectacular blaze. If he felt even more devilish, he would throw something out of the darkness and knock over one or two lamps. Then the tunnel seemed to be on fire!

A Bumpy Ride. The Tunnel Gang were employed cleaning out drains, packing sleepers or changing a sleeper or two. They might even be called upon to replace a rail. One day, when the track was being lifted with jacks, and a flagman was on duty to caution trains, a train took them by surprise. There was no time to remove the jacks. "To the crew of yon train, it must have been like going over Mount Ararat. The driver stopped lower down and asked the ganger: 'What's ta playing at?' The ganger bluffed it out, saying: 'Thou were doing 50 miles an hour. Didn't thou see t'slack further back?' He persuaded the driver that he was in the wrong. The driver was so upset, he pleaded with the ganger not to report him."

Windblown. When the crew of a northbound train had cleared Blea Moor tunnel, the first thing they noticed was the "cemetery" on the left. There was a morbid curiosity in that tract of ground with the "tombstones" rising from it (they were actually boundary markers). There followed a small cutting and, suddenly, the train was on Dent Head viaduct and the footplate men had an unrivalled view of the valley of the Dee.

The fireman of a Derby 3, which had quite a space between engine and tender, was sweeping up between bouts of shovelling when a fierce wind caught him and he was blown across the tender. He collided with a handle which did at least prevent him from being blown clean off the engine. The driver, Old Mattock, turned when he heard the winded fireman grunt and wondered what all the fuss was about.

Dent Head

While crossing Dent Head viaduct, which has a length of 177 yards, and is situated high above the valley, there is a splendid view of Cowgill and Dentdale, with the Howgill Fells providing a backdrop. The Dent Head signal box was brought into use in 1898 and closed in 1965.

A Presence. Ian Ibberson, Inspector of Works at Denthead Viaduct when there was a waterproofing project, sat by himself in the temporary office. The day shift was over and the men had left. He was expecting the arrival of the night shift. It was a still November evening and a good fire was blazing from the day's refuse. Ian gazed idly through the fire to the embankment beyond when a spectre materialised. He felt his hair stand on end. His spine chilled as though it had been stroked by an icy finger. Not far away was an area where, reputedly, railway navvies were buried in unmarked graves. As quickly as the ghost arrived, it departed, leaving only the remnants of smoke clearing – a willow bush.

Hit by Lightning. Norman Dobson was in Dent Head box during a severe thunderstorm in the 1930s. A "thunderbolt" fell at the door of the platelayers' cabin on the up-line side, quite near the box. At the moment of impact, a blue flame or light seemed to run the length of the instrument shelf. There was a faint jangle of bells. Norman was also to remember a smell of sulphur. Most of the instruments in the box were affected. The dog teeth of the arresters on the phone connections were blackened.

Dent Station

From the bridge near Dent station, in clear weather, the eye can trace the line of the railway to the big viaducts of Arten Gill and Denthead. At over 1,000ft, this is the highest mainline station in the land. It was also the place where snow problems were most acute. Despite the presence of snow-fences (upreared sleepers) the deep cuttings filled up in a relatively short time.

No Dog Collar. The experience of driving a car from the valley of the Dee to Dent railway station is almost akin to using a lift. The road climbs six hundred feet in next-to-no time. Jack Sedgwick, for many years signalman at Dent, referred to the worst bit as the Zig Zag. At Dent, snow fences, composed of wooden sleepers standing on end, and now at crazy angles, recall a vain attempt to manipulate the weather.

The signal box where I often met Jack was made redundant and the woodwork was put to the torch. A signalman had been expected to wear collar and tie, "but we kept these in a locker and reached for them when we saw an inspector approaching the box." When Bishop Treacy, an outstanding photographer of trains, paid the first of many visits to Dent, Jack had no idea of his high church position. "He used to say he enjoyed listening to Dent box talk before the men found out he was a parson."

A Porter's Life. In 1934, when Jack Sedgwick became a porter at Dent, he was relieved to have the job, for there was little work available in the dale. Matthew Haygarth was the coal agent at Dent and in the early 1930s Jack had his first experience of life at Dent station when he visited it for a load of coal for the home farm. Coal arrived from the Yorkshire pits in wagons which were put into a siding. Otherwise, coal was loaded from the places where it had been dumped. The road was then surfaced with loose stones rather than tarmac.

Wartime Mystery. When Sandy (Mr Sanderson) was Stationmaster at Dent during the Second World War, he was roused by telephone early one morning and it was reported that a freight train on the up-line had a wagon on fire. He made arrangements for the train to be stopped at Dent, the offending wagon disconnected and put in the siding and the rest coupled up. This was done. The burning wagon had been between two closed wagons and when Sandy was attending to them before the train moved off, he shone his lantern – for it was still dark – on each in turn and saw they were labelled "Explosives." The sheeted wagon that was the cause of the alarm was found to contain the remains of burnt straw. The mystery remains. Could it have been a case of potential sabotage?

Free Bunnies. Also during the war, Sandy had a gun and used to go out shooting rabbits on the areas of land adjacent to the railway. The farmer on the Cowgill side offered to give him cartridges (which then cost 2s.6d for 20) if he would shoot his rabbits. Rabbit burrows were becoming a nuisance to his stock. Sandy gave the rabbits to the footplate men and guards of trains stopping at Dent. They bore them triumphantly to Carlisle or Leeds.

Inclement Weather Problems. One winter – a very bad winter, as they all seemed to be when Sandy was at Dent – the up-line was blocked from Kirkby Stephen to Horton-in-Ribblesdale. Sandy knew from previous experience there might be drifts up to 20 ft deep in cuttings. Sandy had seen trains

buried completely, "engines and the lot," so that passengers had to be dug out and taken to the cabin near the signal box and revived with hot drinks and sandwiches. With the snow ploughs in action, single-line working was possible on the down-line.

Sandy went to Ribblehead, using an up-train on the down-line, and considered that a drift at the approach to the north portal of Blea Moor Tunnel was not as bad as it had been. The snow was not too deep at Arten Gill. The plough might clear both obstructions and re-open the up-line to Blea Moor and Ribblehead, which would shorten single-line working to the stretch north of Dent.

The process began. At Arten Gill cutting, he saw wires flying about the engine cab and there was a bang from the rear snow plough as though it had hit some obstruction. They must keep up speed, so it was ignored. "We entered Blea Moor tunnel and came under the first air shaft. Here there was a crashing sound, the glass in the cab was broken on the fireman's side and ice or glass was flying about all over the place." Since the up-line had been closed, enormous icicles had formed at the bottom of the air shafts in the tunnel. A gang had to be summoned to clear them.

Sandy decided the snow ploughs would return on the down-line. Meanwhile, he walked to Denthead box to advise the signalman what was to be done. As he was crossing Denthead viaduct, he realised (with a profound shock) from marks in the snow that the speeding train had been alternatively running on the track and becoming air-borne. He chilled at the thought of what would have happened if they had come off the road, which would have been a simple thing on a curved line.

The signalman at Denthead had lost contact with the outer world. The bang experienced early in the trip was from the train running over a fallen telegraph pole, which was now smashed to bits. There was tangled wire everywhere. What remained of the pole was tipped down an embankment and the tangled wires cleared before trains could run again.

Off the Rails. A passenger train was de-railed as it came out of Rise Hill Tunnel, the driving rod having buckled and stuck into the ground between sleepers. Sandy went to the scene and found the firemen and the guard were doing their duty and protecting the front and back of the train. It was in late spring, so the passengers were not likely to be chilled. The carriages were collected by a locomotive sent from Carlisle and a crane from Skipton lifted the heavy driving rod and restored the engine to the rails.

A Royal Occasion. Queen Elizabeth (now the Queen Mother) spent a night in the Royal train drawn in at Dent. Next morning, when the train was due to travel south, policemen stood on bridges and men were stationed at every shaft on Blea Moor. At Ribblehead, a few cows that had "come off t'pick-up t'neet afore" broke out and wandered down the tracks towards Salt Lake. "We had to run after 'em... We got 'em back just afore t'Royal Train landed."

Frost-bitten. In 1947, a contingent of the East Lancashire Regiment, billeted at Preston, were summoned from huts at around 3a.m. and marched to the railway station. They entrained in a rake of ice-cold, non-corridor carriages for Rise Hill. Their task was to dig out the line where the water-troughs were to be found. Divided up into gangs, they went as far as the tunnel, loading snow on to low-sided wagons that were towed by locomotive to the nearest viaduct, where it was tipped over the parapet. The work was done by 4p.m. Donald Alker, who was a corporal, cadged a lift on the locomotive of the train mustered for the return journey. As he stood on the footplate, he removed his great coat with difficulty. The coat stood up by itself in the tender.

During the Big Snow, said Dick Fawcett, "they were that short o' men they asked for signalmen and others all the way down to Lancaster and Morecambe to give a hand out of hours. They ran a special train for anyone who could shovel. Our job was to help the platelayers load snow from the cuttings into wagons. When we came into Dent Head cutting, which they had cut through, a man shouted for us to keep our heads in. The snow on either side was that high you could see marks on it left by the carriage doors."

Curiosity. An uncle of Jack Sedgwick, who for many years was signal-man at Dent, was killed through an unusual accident as the train in which he was travelling entered Rise Hill Tunnel. There was a Dent parson with a "spare woman" in an adjacent compartment. Richard was looking out of the window, intent on seeing what they were doing, when he hit his head on the tunnel end.

Garsdale Water Troughs

The water-troughs just south of Garsdale, the highest in Britain, were 1,670ft long, shallow at each end and about six inches deep in the middle. Their capacity was between 5,000 and 6,000 gallons. The water feeding the troughs was stored in a 43,000 gallon lineside tank that at one time was steam-heat-ed in winter. A train in need of water lowered its scoop and lifted it up when the tank had filled, which was not as easy as it sounds. In winter the Garsdale gang had to pick ice from between trough and rail. The ice had to be kept below rail level or there might be a train "off the road."

The troughs were indicated by a white cross in a black box, the source of light being a paraffin lamp. "It always seem to be lit. It must have been well insulated against the gales. When you saw the cross, you dipped the scoop. It either filled or it didn't; you got what you could and then pulled it out." If the train was double-headed, agree-ment had to be reached. "You took one half, and he took the other half."

Footplate men used to say of the troughs that they were frozen for three months in winter, dry for three months in summer and blocked with leaves for three months in autumn. It was only in springtime a crew had any chance of topping up the tender with water. Yet men like Jimmy McClelland, of Carlisle, who had experience of several north-country troughs, including Gretna, pronounced those at Garsdale to be good.

"If you put a Duchess down 'ten tons', it meant that the scoop was right in the trough. You can just imagine the force of water when you are travelling at, say, seventy miles an hour. When you come to near the top, you couldn't let it out. So what you had to do was to 'skim'. Set it for nine and a-half tons till you felt the water gripping it. You watched your gauge. If you didn't get it out in time, it overflowed and you lost 500 gallons of water. On a night-sleeper, you went from Leeds, watered at Skipton, and drew water from the troughs at Garsdale on the way to Carlisle."

At Garsdale, a reservoir that had been made half a mile up the fell-side was the source of the water used in the troughs. Cleaning it out in summer, when the feeder beck was low, proved to be a pleasant job for the local gang. They might let off most of the water – and collect a few trout. When water in the tank was heated by a steam pipe extending from a boiler in the tank house, a man stayed there all night to stoke up the fire.

The permanent way men had plenty of coal for their cabin. "If the tank of a passing engine was over-full, then surplus water washed cobs of coal from the tender. Lids were supposed to be chained down, but sometimes there was no chain. The lids went everywhere. There was an art in working with double-headers. When you were in a pilot, assisting a train, you let the train-man dip first. Then half way across, you'd dip. If it was done the other way round, the train-man didn't get any water."

At the approach of Garsdale, the driver would grunt: "OK, gerrit in." And down would go the scoop. A fireman who served with Old Mattock recalls: "I put the scoop right down, but then gave it a half

turn back. I had my eyes on the water gauge, which was right in front of me. As soon as it was showing three-quarters full, I started pulling the scoop out. Some drivers said you'd missed some water and you might have gone some more. If the tender over-flowed, they were just as ratty. You couldn't win."

Big Bass Telford, a driver living at Carlisle, was asked to plough the area of the troughs, which were frozen solid and covered with packed snow. Bass drove the locomotives hard, hit the snow at speed and instead of going into it the plough rode on to the top of the drift, the locomotives following it. They came to a halt, crossways, on both main lines, about four feet from the bank, which led steeply down into the valley.

Garsdale and Hawes

The station has had several names, including Hawes Junction and Garsdale. The Wensleydale branch operated from a platform to the right of the island (looking north). Garsdale had a celebrated turntable on which locomotives were at the mercy of strong winds. Eventually, it was ringed by a fence composed of sleepers. In view of the generally inclement weather, the passengers waiting on the island had the protection of a ridge and furrow canopy.

Widow's Mite. In the prolonged frosts of 1929, when the condition of the track led to concern, Simon Fothergill and others were flagging [cautioning] at viaducts to ensure the trains had slowed down. He had no cabin or fog hut to shelter him. He contracted pneumonia and died. Simon lived at Moorcock Cottages. Any permanent way men who were in need of lodgings were first directed to the home of his widow. The lodging money augmented her small income.

Round and Round. Early turntables were fitted at each end with small balance wheels. These lifted off when the locomotive was precisely in balance. The driver eased it back and forth until balance was achieved. Then the two members of the footplate crew literally pushed a hundred tons of locomotive and tender around. When stopped, it must match up the rails precisely. Later, a refined turntable had two cranked handles. They worked gearing. Later still, a fitment was introduced that coupled up to the locomotive vacuum pipe and used its power to turn the table. In the early 1950s, this was considered the height of luxury.

Hay and Taties. Garsdale handled a lot of freight, including loads of hay and farm potatoes from Lincolnshire that were needed by local farmers for their stock. The cold earth of Garsdale did not yield enough fodder for them to see the winter through. A former guard recalled: "I have seen a whole trainload of hay from Skipton being split up so that some went to Bentham, some was for Clapham and some was sent up the Drag to Garsdale."

Hard Cash. Richard Fawcett, a Grade 2 mason, began his railway career on the renovation of Dandry Mire viaduct in the 1930s. He received 48s a week. "Back-end was coming and the wind used to blow up Garsdale and bring with it a lot of wet. I was in a cold shop. I was married. There was a house available at Moorcock Cottages if I took a job with the Slip and Drainage Gang. I couldn't see the mason's work lasting so I transferred. My wage fell to 40s. I got a shilling rise. I was off sick and told one of my old mates to keep a shilling back because I hadn't told my wife about it and I wanted that for spending money."

Home Comforts. Moorcock Cottages were palatial compared with the average country cottage, though there was only one decent paraffin lamp in the house and the folk went to bed by candlelight. The company did not provide the cottagers with coal "but we got plenty off the railway." Coal was shaken (in some cases thrown) off the passing engines. Every platelayers' cabin had a big heap composed of coal the men had picked up on the track. There was no water. "We had to carry water from a spring under the fourth arch of the viaduct." Ted Wilson, who occupied the end cottage of the six was paid to empty the earth-closets. The rate was half-a-crown per toilet per month. He wheeled the effluent across the road in a barrow and tipped it here and there in a field. Then his hens would start "scrattin'" among it.

The Tank House. It was used for dances and an adjacent wheelless carriage was the refreshment room. Dick Fawcett never went to a dance in his life. "I was all for country life – out with the gun. I'd go to Moorcock Tunnel. In those days, you could get a blackcock at the side of the tunnel and a red grouse on the land above it any time. I've been in the Tank House when it was all set up and everybody was black-wet with sweat and going mad with dancing."

Picking-up Time. Steam specials did not always run to plan. When the *Great Marquis* provided the traction, the train was drawn to a halt at Long Preston, but no tanker had arrived to replenish the water supply. This being Sunday, with no other trains imminent, the driver of the train, stopped at Settle. He knew where in the yard a hydrant was to be found. Water hoses were coupled together, connecting hydrant to the tank on the engine. By the time the fire brigade arrived, the tank was full. An hour had been lost.

As the train was going through Blea Moor Tunnel, the driver inquired about the state of the water and was re-assured. There was plenty to last until Appleby, where it had been arranged a tanker would meet the train. It was decided to cut the Garsdale stop. There was a tanker standing on the platform at Appleby to give us sufficient water to take the special to Carlisle. The Border City was reached ahead of time. On the Monday, the chief inspector at Crewe phoned up and asked for an explanation. How was it possible for a train that was an hour late at Settle to arrive early at Carlisle?

Hawes

The Wensleydale Railway connected Garsdale with Northallerton. The line was closed but enthusiasts of the Wensleydale Railway Association are hopeful that it will be operational once again. Meanwhile, Hawes station and goods shed have been transformed into a Folk Museum.

Relief. When the Settle-Carlisle was blocked by snow in the 1930s, the Garsdalians were almost at the point of running out of food when it was decided to send a locomotive with a snow plough down to Hawes to replenish the stock. The turntable at Garsdale was "blocked up" so a dozen men who had been sheltering in t'brake van were roused, put on their top coats and dug the turntable out. "It was blowing like the divvil." Said one of the men concerned. "The engine was turned, we got on t'track and managed to get t'points over and set off. We were on North-East and we weren't supposed to be there. Some geese that had been cowering in a hole in t'middle o' t'four foot had their heads chopped off. Later, I went to collect 'em, but they'd gone. Somebody had taken them."

A Wily Ganger. Old Adam, a ganger on the Hawes branch, was a big man who became a legend in his lifetime. Adam had a cabin at t'end o' t'platform at Hawes. A permanent way inspector with a suspicious mind was always creeping down ditches, trying to catch men idling when they should have been hard at work. Adam was fond of saying that he had a good defence against such intrusion. "When I'm in t'cabin, I've got place that hot an inspector couldn't bide to hold t'sneck." He also had a gun with a bent barrel. It was so designed to shoot round corners.

Adam was transporting boards on a platelayer's bogey when the situation got out of control. The boards were sleepers, each sawn into two. Adam had 20 or 30 of them loaded and he "sat at t'front wi' t'handbrake, chewin' bacca." He had eight passengers. "It's a heck of a gradient down to Hawes. We could feel that bogey going faster and faster. We got to t'other end of t'tunnel, and t'auld load was 'jeddering' and sleepers were slipping. First one man, then another, jumped off. You could tell Adam had a panic on, but he wouldn't admit it." He couldn't stop the bogey because the brake wouldn't hold it. "That bogey went right through Hawes station. When it stopped we had about five boards left on. There were also four of us, not nine. We'd boards all the way from t'tunnel, but Adam nivver turned a hair."

A Thrifty Chap. Richard (Dick) Fawcett, born at Sedbusk, near Hawes, joined the railway in the 1930s and worked in Hawes station for a while. He recalled that when one of the signalmen broke his leg, he did not want to lose any overtime, so they wheeled him down to the box in a wheelbarrow. He was a Methodist, "a thrifty chap who was married in a frock coat and had it altered from time to time as the years went by. He was still using it now and again when he died in his seventies."

Bonnyface. As a temporary goods guard at Hellifield for a year or two, Dick many times worked the afternoon passenger train named Bonnyface into Hawes. He had "a nice rest" going. All the quarrymen travelled on Bonnyface then, and it was said it got that nickname because when it turned up they smiled; they were going home. On the return from Hawes, Dick brought the shunt back [he worked the pick-up train to Skipton]. "I used to panic. There was Horton to shunt and I didn't know the quarry traffic. Then you got to Settle. They wanted a cattle truck putting here for morning. They wanted a wagon in the shed. A coal merchant wanted his empties removed." Nearly everything was moved by rail. "That's why you get such lovely clover on the embankments; it came from hay that was being transported in the wagons."

Settle-Carlisle in Action

Photographed by Peter Fox

Black 5 at Aisgill

Above: A Carlisle-bound Class 40 locomotive near Settle, early 1980s.
Below: Leander (5690) on the turntable at Steamtown, Carnforth, prior to hauling a northbound Cumbrian Mountain Express. 1980.

Above: A Class 47 locomotive on a Leeds to Carlisle train, 1983.
Below: The author and resident engineer Tony Freschini "under the arch" at Ribblehead viaduct during restoration work, 1989.

Above: Green Arrow (4771), one and a-half hours late, appears from the mist at Garsdale. *Below:* An engineer's special at Dent while securing a film record of the entire line, 1990.

Above: The distant signal and Blea Moor being approached by Leander (5690), hauling a Cumbrian Mountain Express.
Below: A Black 5 (5305) en route from hauling specials in Scotland is seen near Garsdale. The driver was Cyril Patrickson.

Above: 264T (80080) shunts coaching stock in a rare appearance at Kirkby Stephen, 1993.
Below: The Appleby gang on re-laying work at Kirkby Stephen.

Above: An early method of watering steam engines at Appleby, 1980s.
Below: Taking on water from new tank and crane at Appleby, 1990s.

Above: The driver of Princess Margaret Rose (462) poses with an 0-gauge model of the same locomotive. *Below:* Carlisle receives a driver-training special from Kirkby Stephen.

Aisgill

It was no easy job keeping up a head of steam on the Drag until, at Aisgill, the climb was over. "If they got balked at Settle Junction, they'd grumble and grumble. It could put 40 minutes delay on at Aisgill. You'd find they were slowing up a bit at Stainforth and then you'd get another decent bit o' steam at Helwith Bridge. To keep steam up and go up the Drag at 60 and 70 miles an hour was a miracle."

On the Border. When Jack Maunders, a signalman at Aisgill, was married in 1927, there was the unusual situation for his bride of having a husband working at a signal box in Yorkshire and the home being situated 200 yards away, across the county border in Westmorland. She presided over a railway cottage in which there was no running water except that which ran off the roof into a barrel. A wash-house stood across the yard. A pair of lapwings nested at the edge of the moor, where she hung her washing. She had to pay a penny a year to the landowner for every stoop put in place to support a washing line.

Carved Stones. In the year 1935, Richard Fawcett and his father-in-law, who lived at Aisgill Cottages, visited the so-called Jew Stone, erected by an eccentric who lived at a fine house near the Eden below Carlisle. He traversed the Eden and carved a stone (in various languages) to commemorate the exploit. The name Jew Stone was given by people who could not understand it and a party of navvies, at the time the Settle-Carlisle was constructed, came across the stone and senselessly broke it into pieces. "We once hunted about and found it. Father-in-law gathered up the pieces so they might be seen better.

Not far away, towards Mallerstang Edge, is a quarry where they made gravestones. We went one Sunday and carved our names on some of them with hammer and chisel. There's any number of gravestones, ready dressed, in t'quarry yonder." Millstones were quarried high on Wild Boar Fell. "About half way down there's a beauty, but it had been bogged and when I last saw it there was just a lile bit show-ing."

Not Just a Signalman. Reference has been made to the profitable pas-times of signalmen on the Drag. "They'd do owt to mak a bob or two." The old Midland company was not keen to have its staff doing other work. They wanted a hundred per cent of their effort. One signalman bred fell ponies and contrived to move them about by rail without rousing suspicion. Mallerstang had a signalman who was a chemist. He had a nervous breakdown and moved into the dale. When he had recovered sufficiently, he began work on the railway. The other signal-man, Harry Cowen, was a freelance gardener and mason, his main customer being Dr Gibson, of Kirkby Stephen. Charlie Mecca collected a bit o' scrap or would buy an old car, do it up and sell it for a profit.

At Kirkby Stephen, signalman George Pickering mended watches. Laurie Heslop, at Crosby Garrett, made extra brass from rabbiting. As did Johnny Lothian. A signalman at Griseburn spent his spare time with horn and hazel, being a crook-maker of note. Frank Ridding, of Ormside, mended shoes and, during the war, received a special allo-cation of leather. "The old drivers from Leeds would sling a pair of shoes off as they were going by with a little note – 'back on the 10-55' – and Frank would have the shoes repaired, soled, heeled and stud-ded if required, for 12s.6d." His mate was a keen fisherman who sold his catch. The Appleby signalmen were just gardeners. "Further down the line they didn't seem to have many hobbies."

Mallerstang

The railway runs on a shelf cut from the lower flanks of Wild Boar Fell, high above Mallerstang, which has been described as "the cradle of the River Eden." The stretch of line in Mallerstang was notable for its cuttings, culverts and Birkett Tunnel, which is 424 yards long and was provided with a brick arch ring throughout.

A Hanging Matter. A Carlisle driver of a special, the *City of Wells*, commonly known as the Volcano because of the amount of smoke she issued, took her south to Skipton, passing what was known as Hangman's Hut, where a platelayer was said to have hanged himself. One story was that the hut, a wooden structure with a brick chimney, was demolished to break the link with the tragedy. Jimmy McClelland, the man who drove the *City of Wells*, had a different tale. "We got to Skipton, where I was relieved. There was a special diesel going to Carlisle so my mate and I got a life back with this train. I was up with the driver, who said: 'Have you seen Hangman's Hut, Jimmy?' He replied that he had seen it that day. 'It's not there any more', said the driver of the diesel train, adding: 'You set fire to it'."

Door to Door. Brian Hayton recalls a summer's afternoon "up by Mallerstang" when, as fireman on a train heading for Leeds, he was confronted by "a big lump of coal." It was blocking the shovelling plate. He "pulled it out of the chute on to the shovelling plate. I knew there was a platelayers' cabin between Mallerstang and Aisgill. I saw the cabin, opened the door, pushed the lump of coal with a foot. It went bang on to the ground and split into two bits. One went down the bank. Another went right through the cabin door. And there were platelayers inside. I was scared stiff. I thought I'd hurt somebody."

Culverts Galore. When a culvert in Mallerstang was blocked on the top side, a lake began to form. It was feared that the weight of water might wash away the bank, so two men with tilly-lamps went to free the obstruction. They began to prod the flood debris and suddenly realised the whole lot was beginning to move. They had just cleared the ladder that led to the surface when "t'weight o' watter and all slush shoved the ladder off the wall. We were covered wi' muck from head to foot."

The Mallerstang stretch included the Golden Culvert, so-named because it was truly big, costly to make and costly to maintain. The culvert dealt with water pouring off Wild Boar Fell. The Works Department was concerned with such matters but in the case of the Golden Culvert everyone seemed to get involved.

Summat to Eat. Ernest Jarvis, a driver who lived at Skipton, was familiar with wild weather in Mallerstang. One snowtime, during the Second World War, when he was driver on a munition train from the Hawes branch, the snow was heaped so high he walked straight into the Mallerstang signal box. "You could see no valley. I asked a signalman how he was going on for a relief. He told me it was his third day in the box. 'How is tha going on for grub then?' 'They're sending it up'. I said: 'Oh, we'll have a share wi' thee'. He said: 'You can have what you like'. So we had some sandwiches and a couple of Oxo cubes and some snow watter, and that were that!"

The Eden Valley

To the north of Kirkby Stephen, moors and pastures give way to arable land. The Eden Valley widens like a fan. The train moves under a big sky, with a blue-grey range of hills, the northern Pennines, providing a decisive end to the view eastwards. When the regular stopping train was steam-hauled, and when every station was bustling with life, there was an at-oneness with the landscape which is not apparent in these sealed-in, diesel days.

Redstone Stations. In the summers of years ago there were warm golden evenings, the hue coming from field upon field of ripening grain. In the slack air, it was possible to travel with the carriage window lowered and with a rural tang in the nostrils. Most of the Edenvale stations had truly rural settings. There seemed to be so many stations! No sooner had a train built up speed, and the familiar tattoo of wheels against short track lengths begun to exert its soporific influence on the passengers, than the brakes were being applied once again. I would look out to see a platform and some redstone Midland Gothic buildings come into view.

There was the stationmaster, with smart uniform, "scrambled egg" on the neb of his cap, supervising the flurry of activity. Passengers alighted. Others embarked. Small items of "goods" were transferred. And off we moved, for another mile or two. The names of stations might be recited as in a litany, including Long Meg and Newbiggin, Culgaith and Langwathby, Little Salkeld, Lazonby and Armathwaite.

Kirkby Stephen

The station is about one and a-half miles from the town. Its importance was recognised by the Midland when they provided the station with a range of large buildings. The name has been changed from time to time and once had the cumbersome title of Kirkby Stephen and Ravenstonedale.

Runaways. Jack Holme, who took up railway work in the 1920s, eventually became a guard. His most anxious moment was at Kirkby Stephen, when a locomotive and four wagons were hooked off so that some cattle wagons could be collected. The brakes of the remainder of the train were not sufficient to hold the immense weight. Jack had a gruelling time in the van when it and the wagons went through catch-points, down a bank, through a wall and into a field. The jarring caused him nervous shock. He was off work for a month.

Domestic Stock. The farm man for Leonard Bousfield, of Gorton House, in the middle of Kirkby Stephen, took a drove of cattle up the main street towards the Midland station, one and a-half miles away. A lady who had just finished scrubbing her doorstep left the front door of the house wide open. A cow entered, walked down the passage, turned in the kitchen and simultaneously deposited a heap of quaking dung. The farm man, who stuttered, said: "B-b-b-sharp, m-m-m-m-missus, and get it cleaned up; it s-s-sets like –c-ce-cement!"

Another time, also at Kirkby Stephen, a cow saw an inviting open garden gate, walked through it into the garden and through the open front door of the house. There, while attempting to climb the stairs, it was driven back by an irate householder, but not before it had left its trade-mark on the hall carpet. Normally, cattle were kept to their prescribed path, sometimes with the help of youngsters who were friendly with the family of the cattle dealer.

High Wind. A Carlisle footplate man recalls the first time he heard the Helm Wind, which is created when air from the north-east, cooled on its progress up the Pennines, plunges down a 2,000 ft escarpment and encounters the warmer air of the Eden Valley. A bar or burr of cloud, straight as a brush-shaft, is seen above the fells. Turbulent air frolics along the East Fellside from Castle Carrock to Mallerstang.

A driver recalls being sent to Kirkby Stephen to relieve the snow plough and start ploughing. "Coming up the bank, we had the wind to the fireman's side. We got off the relief engine at the station and went to the signalbox. The signalman said: 'I've been up here a good number of years. I've never heard the Helm Wind as it is today'. You could hear it roaring up at Mallerstang. At Kirkby Stephen there was just a slight wind. When you got to Appleby, there was scarcely any wind. It was said t'Helm never crossed the Eden."

Crosby Garrett

Built in a cutting, this attractive Midland station is no more, though the Stationmaster's House survives; it is in private hands.

The platforms were among the longest on the Midland system.

Kits of Milk. When the Express Dairy opened a plant at Appleby, a special milk train from Hawes stopped at Crosby Garrett and collected milk, adroitly handed by the staff in 17 gallon kits. In the 1930s, farmers arriving with laden kits used horses and traps for transport.

Appleby

At the approaches to Appleby is the aforementioned dairy from which milk was transported by rail to London. The station, reflecting in size the importance of the old county town of Westmorland, had the only footbridge over the line until one was provided at Settle in recent times. Appleby is a watering-place for steam-specials, having a smart new water tank.

The Scavenger. In the grim winter of 1947, the footplate crew of a freight train newly-arrived from the south were "famished." The fireman went looking for food. He was away from the station for about an hour. The driver, Ernest Jarvis, related that his colleague "came back with twelve meat pies in a flour bag. Whoever sold 'im them pies hadn't had t'sense to empty all t'flour out of t'bag." The fireman also had a packet of cigarettes, half an ounce of thin twist (for Ernest) and a box of matches. "The signalman shouted: 'Are you about right now?' I said: 'Just about, old lad, but give us time to put a shovel in t'fire-ole and warm up some pies'. I had two pies. T'fireman scoffed [ate] the rest."

Colourful. Norman Dobson recalled a man who in 1922 went to Appleby for an interview, having applied to be a lengthman in Mallerstang. The interview took place in the inspector's office and "he put you through it, mostly for colours, which had to do with signals. The inspector had a long stick around which were wrapped wools of various colours. You had to pick them out – red, green, yellow."

At Work. Railway work could be chancy, for the company was inclined to sack a man towards the end of December, only to re-hire him in early January. Consequently, he never had holiday entitlement. Charlie Allen of Appleby was to have been paid off in that way but he was saved by the bell. So many slips had occurred near the tracks that he was reinstated. Charlie thus became entitled to holidays but did not know about it. And no one told him!

Bill Wilson, of Appleby, the ganger of the Extra Gang for many years, would not produce a birth certificate. The retiring age was seventy, but he hung on until 1927, he was about seventy-four. He was fond of saying that he had worked on the line during the construction period. At the time of his retirement there was only one other member of that Gang and they had worked on slips and drains.

Frankie Middleton, who served the railway at Dent Head, began farming in a small way. A member of the Appleby gang asked him why this was necessary. Frankie replied: "I'd nowt to talk about at dinnertime."

Under Wraps. During the 1939-45 war, a short freight train drew up for water by the "down" platform at Appleby. The train consisted of the locomotive, two fitted freight wagons containing sheeted packing cases, two bogie bolster wagons and a passenger coach (with no lights showing). On the bogie bolsters were what looked like two large torpedoes. The porter climbed on to have a closer look and eased a corner of a wagon sheet aside. An Army officer appeared and ordered the porter to leave. Later, it was said that the strange objects were miniature submarines to be used for secret attacks in Norwegian waters.

Goosy Gander. Calves in sacks might be seen on the platform at a station like Appleby; the wee creatures were to be entrained for Carlisle. Geese and hens were among the livestock consigned from Appleby. A goose was supposed to be in a crate and hens in a basket with a net over the top. Otherwise the railway company might face a charge of cruelty.

Usually, such birds were being sent to the market at Carlisle but

Alan Dugdale told of a man who appeared at the station with a gander in a sack, in which a hole had been cut, so that the bird's head and neck were visible. The man was going to Carlisle and would pay for the goose on his return. It was to be consigned to an address "down South." The porter, fearing what the "cruelty people" might say if they came across the gander in a sack, took decisive action. When the owner returned from Carlisle, he inquired about the goose, heard it had been sent off, as requested, but (added the porter) he thought it best to kill it before despatch. The irate owner said it was required for breeding purposes. Alan added: "I don't know how they sorted that lot out."

Good Health! A couple who were married at Hellifield caught the train for Carlisle and had their wedding breakfast on the train. They were still in their wedding attire – white gown for the lady, frock coat for the man – and when Appleby was reached they asked to be photographed on the footplate. The reward for the crew was a bottle of champagne. It was explained that none of "the lads" could have a drink while on duty. Later it was consumed from best-quality railway plastic cups.

Griseburn Ballast Sidings

From the 1880s until the 1914-18 war, Griseburn stone provided ballast for the railway. The sidings were used for laden wagons that were available for use. When the quarry was closed, the signal box, which had been constructed in 1905, remained as a block-post. The box, which was closed in January, 1981, stood at the half-way point of the Settle-Carlisle.

Sidings and boxes were especially busy in the Second World War. Griseburn, right out in the country, was a good place for a signalman to be. Few people living in the area could have found the place. You could shunt on the up and down lines and in the war many trains were temporarily held in the sidings. A train with engine failure would be backed into a siding for up to three days while a replacement engine arrived.

A guard clambered up the steps of the Griseburn box one night and reported he was with a trainload of American soldiers. He'd been stopped seven times between Carlisle and Grizeburn because soldiers were hanging their coats from the communication cord. As soon as a train stopped, even at remote Griseburn, the Americans wanted to leave it. There was the comical sight of guards running about shouting them back into their carriages and telling them that a train was coming on the other line.

The Americans were generous, throwing off packs of chewing gum, Ovaltine tablets covered in tinfoil and soup in handy packs. One American tossed out a packet containing 200 cigarettes. A guard saw the Yankees firing live bullets from revolvers at rabbits they saw in the fields. "They used to toss us chewing gum, boxes of peanut butter, packs of Chesterfield and Camel cigarettes, at a time when you could not normally get them. It's a wonder that nobody got killed in the rush."

Alan Dugdale, who had a stint as signalman at Griseburn, was fond of recalling the early part of 1947 – a time of excessive snowfall. Alan was lodging at Asby, about three miles from the box. The landlady was wiser than Alan when she told him that if he went to work on a specific day he would not be able to return when his term of duty ended. He decided to go. Shrewdly, the landlady put plenty of food in his box. (Alan recalled that she used to keep pigs for food and had her own hens).

Alan struggled to work through deep drifts, and as he was on the two-to-ten shift he had all morning to get there. He looked out of the box at ten o'clock and saw fresh snow was packed in the cutting. He was marooned in the box for three days and three nights, during which no trains moved and he never went out. He did not suffer, for he could toast himself in front of a good coal fire and ate up the food he had been given. Laurie Heslop and Billy Oliver who were the other signalmen never got to work – but received their wages as if they had.

Newbiggin

This was a bonny little redstone station in a most attractive village. The station was closed but enough of it was preserved in private hands for us to recall its appeal.

Landslip. A thunderstorm at Newbiggin in 1927 caused a flash flood on the high ground above the up-lineside near Williamsgill. The "stitches" in a turnip field that bordered a steep shale-soil cutting bore the excess water and soil down the field and blocked the land drain. Excess water poured into the cutting, scoring the slope and blocking the up-line. Gang 18, at Appleby, were playing football in the dinner hour when news of the blockage was received. They quickly mustered shovels, picks, fire buckets (filched from the Signal Department), naptha lamps and stands. At the cutting, they found the Carlisle gang was already there with their ballast train. The ganger told the Appleby men: "Dun't gar in t'Carlisle Brakes – they'll be full o' fleas."

Culgaith

The Midland did not propose to build a station at Culgaith. They grudgingly conceded when they received letters from local landowners and the vicar of the parish asking that a station should be provided. Instead of doing this on lines similar to other Edenvale stations, they provided a cottage-style building and wooden platforms. Culgaith was closed to passengers in 1970. A signal box controls the crossing.

Tunnels. The normally safe Rotary Block was indirectly the cause of the Waste Bank collision in 1930. A ballast train was working there. The intervening Culgaith tunnel precluded an intermediate flagman giving a visual signal that the "down slow" had left Appleby. The signalman on duty in Culgaith box wished to give the ballast train as good a margin as possible, so he arranged with the flagman that he would wag the up-distant signal, which stood between the two tunnels.

Langwathby signalled an up-freight on line. There was no chance of wagging the distant. The fireman on the passenger train who was driving passed the down-starter at danger. The guard, who was doing his written work, assumed that the signal had come off. Meanwhile, in Culgaith tunnel there was no secondary flagman and no fog signal on the line. If Joe Hogarth had not raised the alarm, the passenger engine would have smashed members of Gangs 201 and 202 to pulp against the down-line tunnel wall. The men worked night and day after the derailed engines had been removed on March 7. Following the incident, trains were running at caution.

Long Meg

The first signal box to be erected in the northern area of the Settle-Carlisle was at Long Meg. The work was lightened by the loan of the steam crane operated by the contractors in the building of Long Meg viaduct.

Unnatural. Long Meg mine was the only gypsum mine adjacent to the railway to have a ghost. A "something" was seen by a Long Marton man

Lazonby Sand Hole

Sidings were installed to extract sand for use at the motive power depots. At one time, about 12 wagons a week were being despatched. The sandpits capacity was increased in 1914. The sand siding came to an end in the summer of 1963.

The Sand Hole provided safe employment for the deaf or partially sighted and, as such, was a useful asset to Carlisle District. Complaints were rare until the demand was stepped up in the 1940s. The Locomotive Superintendent at Crewe, who had a hefty order for sand, in January 1946 wrote out his complaints in the form of a New Year's card: "Dear Nelson: wishing you all the best... and I hope the supplies of sand are free of sods, stones, soil, clay and other foreign objects." A cocoa tin accompanied the card. In the tin were samples of "foreign objects."

Lazonby and Kirkoswald

The Midland engineers planned to have a cutting at Lazonby but instead constructed a 99 yard long tunnel. Lazonby became one of the busiest stations on the line, apart from Appleby. A well-known firm of Cumbrian bakers have established themselves in what used to be the goods shed. Near the station is the Midland Hotel. A bridge carries the line over the road that leads to Kirkoswald.

On the Staff. Alan Dugdale, who began work at Lazonby station as a junior porter in 1942, told me that his wage was sixteen shillings a week, from which two shillings was deducted and twelve shillings handed to his mother. He retained two shillings as pocket money and, with tips, was able to buy a few luxuries such as cigarettes.

Alan's daily routine began when he made the fire in the office. (Every other room had a fireplace that was unsued). Whereas ordinary travellers and schoolboys sheltered in the chilly main waiting room, important people like the bank manager at Great Salkeld, who lived at Carlisle, strolled into the office and stood before the fire for five or ten minutes before their train arrived.

Alan cleaned up the waiting rooms. There were flag floors except in the ladies waiting room, where the wooden floor was covered with lino. He dusted round, dashed out as the first stopping train arrived, took off any parcels, booked them up and then delivered them. The favourite destination was a small shop at the top end of the village. Old Mrs Johnson, who owned it, handed over a thruppenny tip each time a parcel was delivered, so a porter who received three parcels by a certain train was inclined to take them to the shop one at a time.

Those were the days when signal lamps were filled with paraffin and the cleaning and trimming of those lamps were jobs for the signalman. There was a rule that when a lamp had been re-filled and re-lighted, then it must stand ten minutes, to give the flame time to settle down. Any lamp that went out during its term of duty had to be sent to Derby to be examined and there was subsequently a report to ponder over. Before sending it off, John Brunskill, the stationmaster, would ask Alan if he thought it was turned up too high or "Did it stand ten minutes before you took it out?"

Mr Brunskill had been in London for many years. He married a girl from Culgaith and therefore requested that he be moved north. In London, he had been a ticket clerk who dealt with long queues. "He was a marvel with that little ticket machine. You used to push a ticket into the machine and it would click. Then it was turned round and clicked so that it was dated at both ends. When Mr Brunskill was operating it, he worked so fast that you only heard one click."

Dick Harper, who served the company as clerk, became Stationmaster at Newbiggin. If Johnny Graham, the cattle dock man, asked Alan to do anything, he knew from experience it was to be done right away. His figure suggested that he drank a good deal, which was true. He had a job that favoured it, for he was forever going to the Midland Hotel on auction days to meet the dealers.

"He was a good man for the railway because he knew the rates. If he didn't know a specific rate, he'd nip up to the station for details. He'd say: 'There's Mr Nelson from Colne wanting six wagons. There's Kelso there with the wagon. Can we undercut him'." Within a couple of hours there'd be a drove of sheep coming up to the station, their destination being Colne.

Jimmy Bell, the warehouseman, was an exceptionally clean and tidy man. He ensured that the brass handles on the many office drawers were gleaming.

Lord of the Manor. When Sir Gerald Lee, of Lazonby Hall, requested an express to stop at the station, it stopped. The Midland had bought land from the Lee family. The local reaches of the railway were built on it. Sir Gerald had a great enthusiasm for trains. "Every now and again," said Alan Dugdale, "you would hear a shrill whistle as a goods train approached. He would be firing it, with a begrimed and knotted handkerchief covering his head. As he passed through Lazonby station, he would give a friendly wave." He had property in Yorkshire and when he moved down with his family, the gardeners at his Lazonby Hall forwarded each week, via the railway, a large hamper full of fresh fruit and vegetables.

Midland Hotel. Lazonby had the Midland Hotel and what was called The Bottom Pub. At the Midland, there were no facilities for visitors to stay overnight, being – at the middle of last century – a place for drink. "It was classed as just a bit more stylish than the Bottom Pub, but both places were packed out on auction days." Mine host at the Midland was called Smith – Mr Smith. "Anybody you thought had owt was called Mister!"

Sheep and Rabbits. "All these fells right round – Renwick and Glassonby, Gamblesby, Hunsanby, Melmerby – were all big sheep runs. The autumn sheep sales at Lazonby were impressive, with as many as 60 wagons of sheep being sent away from the station on big sale days, for dealers arrived from all over the country. Before the war it was just a matter of taking your sheep to the auction and selling them to the highest bidder. Some of the buyers were from big corporations. A Penrith man bought for Manchester Co-op. He'd tour the pens before the sale and check on the quality. When the Second World War began, instead of weighing them, as they did with cattle, three men were commissioned from the Ministry of Food to grade the sheep. There was a lot of fiddling going on with the grading. It didn't matter what some folk took in, they always got grade one."

In the 1920s and 1930s, several local men made a good living trapping rabbits. The charge for sending a crate full of rabbits (some eighteen couples, equalling a hundredweight) to Bradford or Leeds was 4s.8d. A special rabbit crate would normally hold eighteen couple but an experienced packer might get another ten couple in, hopefully at the same rate. The station staff were soon aware of the crates that had been overloaded.

Looking for Salmon. The "toffs" from Bradford and Leeds who disembarked at Lazonby station for salmon fishing were met by ghillies and accommodated at the Brackenbank Hotel, near Great Salkeld. A man kept one salmon and the other fish were despatched to Edwards & Walden, of London. The firm's name appeared on the special boxes used for this trade.

It's Faster by Pigeon. Several Lazonby men were pigeon-fanciers. One of the favourite ruses of a porter who was keen to make his "homer" fly faster was to introduce a rival bird to make it jealous and inclined to return to the loft at top speed. Even pigeon-fanciers had their failures. The porter had a "tumbler" among his racers. This type of bird flies to a good height, then tumbles in a most spectacular way, pulling out into level flight only when close to the ground. Unfortunately, the porter's "tumbler" usually forgot to pull out and would hit the ground with a sickening thud, knocking itself out. Remarkably, these spills did not prevent it from repeating the exercise.

Armathwaite

The brightest object is a restored signal box. The medium-size station formerly had a larger-than-average array of cattle pens. Red sandstone forms the buildings, as is customary in the Eden Valley.

Consolation. A sub-ganger at Baron Wood was acting as ganger at Armathwaite. So that he would not have to walk through three tunnels, he was instructed to walk to Lazonby and travel to Armathwaite by train. He did this in strict compliance with orders but a light engine travelling from Carlisle to Appleby ran over him and killed him. At the funeral, the inspector comforted his widow as best he knew, saying: "You know, Mrs —, it's no good crying over spilt milk."

Low House Crossing

A level crossing is an unusual feature on the Settle-Carlisle. Here the crossing is on the skew. Lifting barriers succeeded gates in 1975. A celebrated signalman was Alan Dugdale, who had a fund of tales about local railwaymen.

Cumwhinton

This medium-sized station, built of the red sandstone of Edenvale, was closed in November, 1956. A row of four cottages, with two porches (adjacent houses used a single porch) had been constructed by the Midland for their local employees, the stationmaster having a detached house of impressive size.

Mowing the Batters. Bowman Graham and another notable scythesman "tossed up" for the upline or downline side of a fairly equally pitched cutting. At the drop of a hat, they started to mow the batters the full length of the cutting. Norman Dobson recalled they wore clogs with strap-on attachments [crampons] that gave them grip on the steep ground. This partly compensated each man for having one foot at a much lower level than the other. Bowman Graham won the contest. Two of three sets of crampons were to be seen in the tank house at Lazonby.

Carlisle

The Settle-Carlisle line ended at Durran Hill and Petteril Bridge, just south of Carlisle. To the north of the city was Kingmoor, a very large depot, which even in 1955 had eight running roads. When you came out of Kingmoor shed there was a coal plant, where there were various grades of coal, from good to indifferent, thence to the pit where the fires were cleaned.

A Reight Good Fire. The best coal was that emanating from Holbeck, Leeds. They called it "Yorkshire Splint." It expanded with heat. Jimmy McClennand, who was transferred to Carlisle in 1955, recalls when he was "firing" the night-time Waverley from Skipton to Carlisle. The engine was an A4. A tall Leeds fireman said: "I've put a good fire on, old love. She's all reight, tha knaws." When he opened the doors, Jim saw it was full of Yorkshire coal. "I sat down. Do you know where I pitched some coal on? Horton! Even then, everything looked white hot."

In Barracks. Railwaymen dreaded an overnight stay at barracks in the Carlisle area. Each was basic, noisy and usually so crowded that a newcomer might have to wait for a bed to be vacated. Sleep did not come easy at premises that lay close to a busy junction. At Petteril Bridge, where the barracks were a house, a weary footplate crew would arrive at 2a.m., have something to eat and then sit and play cards with the chap in charge. When 6a.m. arrived, he left for home, and the visitors had to make their own beds.

In Close Touch. When the Control came into being at Carlisle, no one visualised its rate of growth. Nor could he imagine how useful it would become. The newly-appointed DC even had time to take a look outside, as at Petteril Bridge, where Bill Davidson was on duty as a goods shunter. Bill misjudged the clearance between two vans, a steel one and a wooden one that was bolted on planks. The steel van collided with the wooden van and sheared off most of the bolts.

It was at this stage that the DC came around the corner. The vans stood in close juxtaposition. "Can you spare a minute?" Bill asked, respectfully, adding: "Do yer think that van's clear?" The DC said: "Yes, Bill, it seems clear to me." Bill said: "That's what I thowt." But it wasn't. When Bill was a novice at shunting, a derailment or buffer-lock had occurred. An attempt to separate the two vehicles was unsuccessful. Said Bill: "Git a bar and payzer, min." What he meant was – prize them apart!

Better Late... When blizzards struck the line, Ernest Jarvis was the driver of the first train, a freight, to get through to Carlisle in three days; the passenger trains had travelled over t'Nor-west, by Ingleton. Ernest and his fireman reached the city at mid-day on the day after they had started the journey. "We landed at the main line, Durran Hill, and I remember laughing at my fireman, wi' his black face. Somebody said: 'Control wants you'. I said: 'They're a bit late in t'day, aren't they?'

"We were told to book on at Kingmoor, but I didn't want to go there. Last time it happened they were puncturing fish tins to see if there were any fit to eat. We'd go into town for a wash and brush-up, for we looked like a couple of chimney sweeps. Then we'd go to the

highest-class restaurant we could find. We heard an express was going from Citadel, on the Nor-west line. We got into t'first coach and afore it got to Lowgill I was fast asleep. We signed off at a quarter to six. That wasn't a bad do, was it? Though I'd had even worst times – down t'pits."

Passed Cleaner. In 1948, when 16-year-old Brian Hayton started as a cleaner at the huge depot of Kingmoor, up to a thousand workers were associated with the place. Apart from the footplate crews, including many from Scotland, there were the back-up men – shed labourers, those attending to the coal elevator and the men who worked at the ash-pit, where engines were cleaned. As a cleaner, with regular hours, Brian's education was mainly Saturday morning talks by his superior, who was keen to emphasise not just what to do but what to leave alone when attending to a locomotive, a prime example being the regulator.

As a past cleaner, on shifts, Brian now spent his time applying diesel oil to begrimed engines. There were four in the cleaning team. One was concerned with the tender, one with the boiler and two with the motions. Brian liked attending to the boiler because it was straightforward work. He did not like doing the motions, the work being fiddly as well as dirty. "Some depots used rape oil that left a nice skin on the paintwork." Sponge cloths were in use, the most resistant dirt being scraped off with a metal appliance that had a sharp end. So did young hopefuls begin their railway careers, removing "oil and grease and muck off the ash-pan, the motions and at the back of the driving wheel, which was always thick with oil."

Having passed as a cleaner, Brian now set his sights on being a fireman. Army service intervened, during which he was booked as a fireman. Back at Carlisle, he retained his memories of cleaning. The first job a budding fireman undertook was throwing fires out at Durran Hill. He had a long-handled shovel and a large pair of tongs with which to remove the bars. "The engines were not bad coming off the Midland because from Aisgill a fireman had not been using much coal. He had levelled off the fire and broken up any clinker." A locomotive arriving from the north usually had its firebox full up. Brian remembers when the rocker-grates were introduced. "They were a doddle. You didn't have to take the bars out." A cleaner would shout, enthusiastically: "Here's a rocker."

Well Tuned. Dick Hutton was working a flyer on the "up" from Carlisle. His locomotive was a Claughton, which seemed "in good nick." Dick had been experimenting with big fires, with medium fires and with various settings of valve openings. It was blowing off at Smardale and running sweetly. "I've cracked it at last," thought Dick. Then – *phiz*, with plenty of dust. He had "dropped the plug" and his loco was incapacitated. Ah well, thought Dick, "back to the drawing board."

The Ash-pit. W C Addy, of Leeds, who was a fireman on the Carlisle route when he was twenty years of age, remembers Kingmoor, Carlisle, as the busiest place he had seen. "You left your engine in one of two rows of engines – a matter of twenty or thirty in all – waiting for a place at the ash-pit where the firebox would be cleaned. It was an hour's job to dispose of a single engine. The footplate crew went into the lodge to have their nine hours off duty. When they returned their engine might only just be getting on to the ash-pit. At Carlisle, Bill Addy met cleaners who were older than his father. They had been 'put back' and their wage rate, at 36s, was proportionately smaller. They were receiving less money than the young fireman, the rate for a fireman being 57s."

Big Bass. David Tibbetts, of Carlisle, who began his railway career in the 1940s, told me of "firing" to Aisgill. A knocker-up arrived at his home with a note to indicate that he must book on at 12.03a.m. to help pilot the Midnight Express. His driver that night was Big Bass Telford, a huge but extremely kind-hearted chap. Bass looked at young David and asked: "Have you ever bin on one of these afore?" David shook his head. Said Bass: "Well, stand over there – out o' t'road, and hang on. Just keep an eye open. If you see a yellow signal, shout to me." And off they set, with David hanging on for grim death and Big Bass shovelling coal and also driving.

David was petrified at what was his first experience of the railway. It was black dark. The loco was a Midland type passenger engine, with no doors. He remembered seeing the dawn about 3 or 4a.m., during the return to Carlisle. Bass was then allowing the young man to do the firing. David was extremely pleased at having helped to pilot the

Thames-Clyde express on its nocturnal dash across the fells. Every fireman developed the knack of frying a meal on his shovel. David was shown how to lay bread and cheese on the wooden seat, heating the shovel, then holding it over the cheese and thereby grilling it. "It was lovely when cooked in this way."

Passing Out. When Brian Hayton, of Carlisle, was passed out as a driver on a steam train, George Gordon took him to Hellifield on a goods train and brought him back on the local, stopping at all the stations, to see how he performed. When the goods trains had loose-coupled wagons, a driver and the guard had to know all the dips and gradients. It's easy now, he said with a smile that nullified his comment. "I think that some of the drivers put an orange on the cab floor and whichever way it rolls they put the diesel power on. If it rolls forward, they shut it off. They're going downhill."

A Coat of Green. In 1970, when "steam specials" were introduced to a line that had been devoid of steam for a decade, Skipton men got *Green Arrow* on Good Friday. Jim MacLennan had the job of driving it back on the Monday. The *Green Arrow*, with its green livery, was to be driven by an LMS man. "The inspector, George Gordon, said to Jim at Carlisle station: 'For goodness sake, when you leave this station, don't slip'. All the old drivers of what had been a rival company would be lined along the platform, watching every movement. When we got to Appleby, the lad who had rebuilt the engine came on to the footplate and revealed he had found the side-rods of the Green Arrow on the back of a tender at Hellifield shed. He rode on the footplate with us from Appleby to Garsdale."

Some Recent Castleberg Books
by W R Mitchell

Birds of the Lake District

This new-style bird book is for the many visitors to the Lake District who are attracted by the birds of mountain, lake or shore and would like to know more about them and their places in England's most astonishing tract of country. The book supplements the standard handbook on birds by concentrating on the most distinctive species. The author, Bill Mitchell, has studied local bird life for over half a century. The illustrator, David Binns, is one of our finest bird artists.

ISBN: 1 871064 64 3   £6.50

Cuckoo Town
Dales Life in the 1950s

ISBN: 1 871064 59 7   £6.50

When the future state of the countryside is being hotly debated, we look back at life in Austwick in the middle of the 20th century when a well-balanced community found contentment in life that is not to be experienced in the brash, media-led world of today. Every page has its tales of characters who lived in the Yorkshire Dales of not-so-long-ago.

Fred Taylor:
Yorkshire Cheesemaker

Fred, born at a remote farm in upper Dentdale, was apprenticed to the land when he was handed a "fixing" shilling by an irascible farmer. His true vocation began after Frank Dinsdale opened a creamery and Fred applied himself to making the celebrated Wensleydale cheese. Dales farmers worried little, if at all, about hygiene, for "milk tastes o' nowt till cow's hed its foot in t'bucket."

ISBN: 1 871064 54 6 £4.99

Other Castleberg Titles

Birds of the Yorkshire Dales	£6.50
Ghost-hunting in the Yorkshire Dales	£5.99
Music of the Yorkshire Dales	£5.99
Sacred Places of the Lake District	£6.50
Beatrix Potter – Her Life in the Lake District	£6.20
The Lost Village of Mardale	£5.60
Garsdale – History of a Junction Station	£6.50
Mile by Mile on the Settle to Carlisle	£5.99
The Men Who Made the Settle to Carlisle	£5.99
Life in the Lancashire Milltowns	£5.99
Nowt's Same	£6.50
You're Only Old Once	£4.99
Mini biographies:	
Tot Lord and the Bone Caves	£4.50
Edith Carr – Life on Malham Moor	£4.50
Edward Elgar in the Yorkshire Dales	£4.99

All **Castleberg** titles are available at good bookshops or, in case of difficulty, please write to: North Yorkshire Marketing, 22 Azerley Grove, Harrogate, North Yorkshire HG3 2SY
We will be pleased to send you a complete list of titles and an order form
No postage is charged on **Castleberg** books